Writers in praise of The S

T0152363

"Moving and provocative, *The Fo....... .... a profound journey into the heart of another culture. What does it mean to teach and be taught? What does it mean to transform and be transformed? Are teacher and student finally, above all, comrades? This memoir—part biography, part autobiography, part portrait of an alchemy—is as transmuting as its subject, and a joy to read."

Gish Jen, author of *The Girl at the Baggage Claim: Explaining the East-West Culture Gap*

"*The Fourth String* is one of the most beautiful memoirs I've read in a long time. And by 'beautiful' I'm not simply referring to its spare, elegant language but to the exceptional beauty of its spirit. This is an insightful and deeply generous book written by a woman as open to surprises within herself as she is to the revelations she discovers about her temporarily adoptive country of Japan. Janet Pocorobba is by turns curious, funny, sensitive, and always, always brave."

Pamela Petro, author of *Sitting up with the Dead: A Storied Journey through the American South*

"*The Fourth String* is a piercingly insightful memoir of a young woman's search for herself by diving into the demanding traditional art form of the shamisen in a country renowned for keeping outsiders at arm's length. With unflinching observation of Japanese society and human relationships, she details her own entanglements with art and self-knowledge."

Liza Dalby is an anthropologist, writer, and scroll mounter

"Exquisitely written ... takes us on a spiritual quest in a new country and culture, ... the soul of a place whose past secures hope and whose present yearns for modernity."

Rachel Manley, author of *Drumblair*, winner of Canada's Governor General's Award for Literature

"Ms. Pocorobba tells an eloquent and insightful story about Japanese music and culture. Her observations shed light on our longing for beauty and purpose. In Japan, she informs us, a child at birth is not age 'zero' but 'one,' which means that the first year is grown into, a shape chosen for her to reach. 'She does not have to become anything that has not existed already.' Ms. Pocorobba's story compellingly explores this paradox: the arduous journey a person must undertake to become the musician or artist she was always meant to be."

Kyoko Mori, author of *Yarn: Remembering the Way Home*

"In this hauntingly beautiful memoir, Janet Pocorobba shows us a world within a world that we've never seen before. This is a Japan where ancient and modern meet, where longing and belonging, foreign and familiar, are searingly depicted within the lives of two women.... Pocorobba's achievement is the subtle way she's transformed how memoir so often only explores the men in mentor. In her hands, narrator and writer alike master complex and completely new notes deep within that most foreign of countries: the human psyche."

Alexandra Johnson, author of *The Hidden Writer*, recipient of the PEN/Jerard Fund Award Citation for nonfiction

"With lyrical prose and elegant precision, Pocorobba tells a gripping story of teacher and student, practice and dreams, and the ways we listen to our own music and discover our true self."

Hester Kaplan, author of *Unravished*

"The intimate, evocative world unveiled in Janet Pocorobba's *The Fourth String* is a compelling place to visit.... An effortless read by a writer who manages the impossible—capturing the ephemeral."

Elizabeth Dowd, Noh Training Project US, Producing Director

"*The Fourth String* transports you into the exquisite minutiae of thoughtful, aesthetically oriented 'gaijin' life in Japan."

Leonard Koren, author of *Wabi-Sabi: for Artists, Designers, Poets & Philosophers*

The Fourth String

A MEMOIR OF SENSEI AND ME

Janet Pocorobba

Stone Bridge Press • *Berkeley, California*

Published by
Stone Bridge Press
P. O. Box 8208, Berkeley, CA 94707
TEL 510-524-8732 • sbp@stonebridge.com • www.stonebridge.com

Photograph of author by Sharona Jacobs.

Cover design by Linda Ronan. Typography and layout by Peter Goodman.

Printed in the United States of America.

10 9 8 7 6 5 4 3 2 1   2023 2022 2021 2020 2019

P-ISBN 978-1-61172-046-4
E-ISBN 978-1-61172-934-4

For M.N. and R.L.,
my listeners,
and for my parents

The Fourth String

Every seed destroys its container or else there would be no fruition.

FLORIDA SCOTT-MAXWELL

PART I

1

... a companion to order and control ...

Sensei existed long before me, as a child on the foggy foul-weathered Sea of Japan, though I have always imagined her sprung whole, like Athena, from the head of Zeus. I am surrounded by pictures of her—at her sink in her old rooms in Tokyo, with the pink gas heater to warm her water to wash dishes; walking alongside the professor under an umbrella in her chic arrow-patterned kimono coat; placing her hand on my shoulder outside the kabuki theater, an unexpected claiming; sitting by a stream in Kyoto in her pinwheel velour Beatles cap, next to where a blue heron stands.

She took me to her childhood home years later, when it was on the verge of being torn down. Out in front of the traditional wooden house was the bench where, as a girl, she ate her lunchboxes alone to escape the interior gloom. She showed me her mother's rooms, which she'd modeled after the Imperial Villa, with papered panels and a glossy stage. Her father's small study with its camera lenses.

"Traveling," she called going out together, even if we were just going across town. "My spirit likes traveling, like yours does...." She saw herself differently with me, I think. I have always felt not quite natural with Sensei, yet completely myself.

That day, walking in an arcade near her house, with no music to plan, no upcoming concerts, we were talking about our pasts. "I was also," she said, "how do you say ... slut?"

Did she say what I think she said? I wanted to believe she was as desperate as I was for love. Had maybe a blizzard of men in her past.

I wonder now if she sometimes said only what she thought I needed to hear. But then again, isn't that what a good teacher does?

≡

Sensei became my teacher, if that is what it can be called, on a hot day in September 1996. All I remember is that, from the start, it felt like something was missing. Off kilter. Not quite what it should be.

And why wouldn't I feel that? I was new to Japan. I had no history with the place, no desire for it until I was knee-deep in debt and needed a way to earn money. English teaching was the answer, and what would bring me to her rooms in Tokyo, and to the shamisen.

Chi chi chi, ton, ten!

It was sweet, it was sour, it snapped, it slid.

She affixed it on my lap with sticky pads that looked like jar grips. She gave me a pick to travel its strings. She sat across from me and we played its tilting, melancholy notes.

"Wait! Space!" she called.

My fingernail split.

Shouldn't there be another note, something to complete it, restore it to balance?

"No," she said. There was nothing. Only *ma*, space, the "live blank" that existed between sounds.

"How can I learn?"

She looked at her hands, as if the answer lay there in flesh and bone.

"You have to steal," she said. "It's the only way."

Her first lesson: no matter how much I was given, only the things that I took would be mine.

≡

I found Sensei in the classified ads of an English magazine, under "Learning" or "Arts," I can't remember which, as she used both, depending which brought more students that week. *Free lessons in shamisen and singing! Take something home with you from your stay in Japan!* That it was so small and sandwiched between other ads made it no less extraordinary, the most radical word being "free." This was usually reserved for old futons or space heaters. And the appearance of the word "shamisen," appearing nowhere else in the hip contemporary magazine, was so unusual that it prompted a friend to cut it out and send it to me. She had circled the ad and written on a Post-It: "I thought you might want to check this out."

So she remembered, I thought. The living room of our dorm at Smith College, in the fall of 1985, our freshman year. I was playing the grand piano in the living room, appreciating the fine keys and action. She was sitting on a sofa in wraparound shades, swinging her room keys around the tall neck of a Rolling Rock beer. On her feet were black canvas high top sneakers, spiking up from her skull was a prickly blond Mohawk. By the end of four years, she had a bob, an art history major, and a job teaching English in Japan. She'd married a Japanese and now worked in an art gallery.

"No matter what you see, it's Japanese underneath," she had told me over tempura on my first outing to Tokyo, where she pointed out that energy drinks contained nicotine, and a bottle of something pearly pink in the supermarket was squid poo.

But at times, she confessed her loneliness, like at a shrine festival that summer, when she gestured to the families in cotton kimono strolling past. "This is when you know you'll never fit in."

I couldn't imagine making a life in such a stark, drab place, such a scrambled city, full of ugly buildings like the school where I worked in Odawara, made of cinderblock, with its plain classrooms where I could not even leave a pair of pumps overnight because of the rules.

Odawara was known for pickled plums, trick wooden boxes, and fish paste. From the veranda of our apartment, you could see its hills ringed in mist, the sparkling sea, the wing of a reconstructed castle roof. On the streets downtown, electricity ran over ground in thick cables trained up like wisteria. The sky was always inflamed, like a hot puffy sore.

I had come to Odawara with my boyfriend Larry, whom I'd met in graduate school in Chicago a few years before. Larry was Southern, soft-spoken, shy. In Japan he refused to bow. "It's undemocratic," he said. I wanted to know how deep to bow, and to whom. He had trouble folding his long lanky frame under lintels and tabletops, and struggled with his cowboy boots in *genkan* entryways. One boy in his class, Tetsu, pointed excitedly to his steel-tipped toes and said, "Dirty Harry."

Two hours south and west of Tokyo, Odawara offered little to do aside from work. I planned outings to nearby temples and shrines, but sometimes it was just as fascinating walking to the stationery store, passing the train station where an old woman grilled skewers of meat on a charcoal hibachi and high school girls ringed their calves with glue to get the perfect slouch on their socks. At a gas station, eight men and women in green jumpsuits alighted on the entering car, as swiftly and intently as dragonflies, to fill its tank, wash its windows, check the tires, and refill fluids, all in one choreographed sweep, then lined up and bowed as the car sped away.

How to explain that these moments of mystery were here before Sensei, and that they only increased after, not to be solved but to be known in all their unknownness?

Larry was everything I could want in a life partner, and this wasn't not on my mind. I was twenty-eight and had given myself until thirty-one to get married, thirty-three for my first child, though I had no idea where those numbers had come from. We were good friends, he was smart and liked to talk, he was trusting and gentle.

These were all good reasons but on the plane over I was already leaning into the window, writing in my journal that I didn't want to be pressured into commitment by a "middle-class spinster specter." I envied a girl in overalls sprawled across three seats, dozing. "I don't know if I ever want to get married," I wrote that first year in Japan.

In the corner of our bedroom sat two backpacks filling rapidly with travel guides, maps, and paperbacks for a trip to Thailand in December, when our teaching contract was up.

At night I wrote stories of invented languages, weird occurrences, a haunted apartment. And the strangest of all, a vision I had on the eve of leaving for Japan: a woman abroad wearing the high collar and long skirts of Victorian dress, sitting at a desk writing letters. She was a friend to the "natives" and spoke their language perfectly. She defended their cause and used her power to earn them equality and protection, to preserve their endangered culture.

I told no one of this vision. It was an Orientalist fantasy, a colonial embarrassment, this portrait of a woman who was utterly and capably alone.

=

The day I met Sensei the mugginess of summer was hanging on. By the time I reached the train in Odawara to take me to Tokyo, I was mopping sweat from my upper lip and wishing I hadn't worn a white oxford. I watched the rice fields as we pulled out of the station and glimpsed Mount Fuji, which could appear suddenly, like a giant looking over your shoulder, but it was cloudy, only its peak transparent like a flat white crayon in the distance.

When I called to respond to her ad, Sensei had instructed me, in her heavily accented English, to transfer to a local train and get off at Setagaya Daita station, which I did, and which had none of the glamour or noise or festivities of even one station away. This Tokyo neighborhood was quiet, with a tofu seller and post office by the turnstiles, and an international grocery with coffee samples spicing the air.

Sensei stood in the foreground of all this, holding the bright green receiver of a pay phone. I had arrived late, and she was calling to see if I had forgotten, she told me later. The toes of her wooden clogs were tilted forward, whether for height (she was very tiny, maybe four foot eight) or as a way to rest her feet, I didn't know. She was in full Japanese gear, which I later learned she donned for first meetings. They expected kimono, didn't they? "Very Japanese-y," she said and laughed.

Royal blue silk of a *ro* weave, so sheer you could see the white underrobe shimmer. A pattern of large flat fans and dolls. Small, well-defined hands. A thumb nearly not there.

And the hair: a thousand inky oiled strands combed into a sharp line at her neck. To call it a bob would be frivolous. This hair was rigid and composed. I admired its precision, its mystery. The vanity of it.

"I am—," she said, and offered me her first name, Western-style. I used her first name, though I have always thought of her as Sensei, "the one who came before."

The truth is I have never quite been able to find the right word for her presence in my life. Nothing seems to cover the enormity of her placement, her importance in all that came then and after. Mentor, monk, mother. She was none and all three. The best word she ever used came one evening at a restaurant where we were having dinner before a performance the next day. In the weeks leading up to a show, Sensei never used kitchen knives for fear of finger cuts.

We were picking at the scanty salad bar, feeling dreamy and expansive in the space between practice and the stage. We had a special relationship, she said. We were "comlets,"

Shooting stars? I thought. OK, sure.

And then I realized, of course, she had misplaced the "r" for "l."

The word she meant was "comrades."

=

At the station, she pointed down a small slope. A small purse looped around her wrist. I couldn't help but think she was playing dress up, like a small girl in her mother's closet. And I wouldn't be exactly wrong. Something from the start about her rang out as grand performance and also absolutely true.

We walked along a busy road with four lanes of traffic roaring by in both directions. Bicycles rang their bells as they careened past. Her wooden shoes rasping the pavement, Sensei clipped along evenly, holding onto the side curtain of her hair in the gusts, squinting up at me, as if from a sandstorm.

Why was I in Japan? What were my plans? Why did I want to learn Japanese music?

This continued a line of inquiry begun on the telephone. She was serious about music, she had said. "We should enjoy." Already it was attached to a philosophy.

It was hot. Everything was gray, the buildings, the sky, the people in their somber clothes. Only Sensei was colorful, like a butterfly in their midst. Whether it was true or not, as we walked the traffic softened a little, and the drabness of Tokyo was tempered by her friendship, her gentle but insistent presence at my side.

At a lone cherry tree, she turned left into what looked like a motel complex of three-story concrete buildings with long verandas. She had won her rooms in a government lottery, I would learn, after her divorce. I followed the drawl of her clogs up the stairs to the right.

"How often did you practice piano?" she asked as we arrived at door #105. She slid a key from her obi. ("To be a woman is to be always hiding something," I read once.)

I looked at an empty ramen bowl sitting on a tray outside a neighbor's door.

"A couple hours a day," I said. I had always wanted to practice that long.

"Thinking and doing are not same," she would say later whenever I was dreaming up some big thing I was going to do. Shake her head as to a small child. "Totally different."

=

Inside it was dusky and felt like evening. She dropped her shoes and stepped up into the rooms, sighing, as if she'd just lugged a bag of heavy groceries up the stairs. She went around turning on overhead fluorescent lamps that cast a sickly glow. I heard the ticking of a gas flame as I unlaced my shoes and stepped up.

She came to the center of the room and clasped her hands as if to deliver dire news. "Shamisen music is disappearing and Japanese people do not care."

Small talk did not seem to be part of her vocabulary.

I found her seriousness almost a performance in itself. There was an orchestrated quality about it all, and about her life, too. I didn't know if she'd be young or old, married or single. I'd imagined, in fact, a blue-haired old lady with a husband snoring in the corner. But as she prepared our tea and moved us to more serious matters— music—she seemed entirely herself.

The apartment was three small rooms and a bathroom sealed off by an accordion door, above which hung, askew on its hook, a framed portrait of the Madonna and Child. The kitchen floor was brown linoleum, the walls, cracking concrete. It was old but clean. Polished, even. A small fold-out table on wheels held a black lacquer bowl that reminded me of her hair. Piled high were rice crackers in silky packages and bags of potato chips.

Instead of assembling at the table, she led us into the rooms, carrying two steaming cups on a tray. The room between the kitchen and music room was empty. The floors were smooth as a stage, and the sun was coming in off the back veranda, which opened onto an overgrown garden and the exhaust fan in the back of the family restaurant next door.

She paused at the threshold of the next room and let out a little puff of air. "My sanctuary."

The doors between rooms had been removed and so it gave the impression of an approach, a region of delay, empty passage to buried treasure. For every corner and shelf of the room was filled with music. Scores, concert programs, photo albums, cassette tapes, CDs. Higher up were books, including the Edo Encyclopedia she referred to when teaching and photocopied drawings from to line our scores. Along the walls hung several shamisen, their sound boxes covered with silk pouches, some cut from the sleeve of an antique kimono. Tanned faces of drums lined the shelves, bamboo flutes perched in baskets.

I wouldn't take it all in for years, when I would know what was in all the drawers, where to expect her to reach for a pencil or extra pick.

Two objects lay on the table under cotton towels. She whisked the towels away dramatically. "Say hello to shamisen."

I was surprised at how unattractive the instrument looked, how odd. The smooth fretless neck was too long. The sound box was too square. Three tuning pegs stood out at the top like careless hairpins.

"Primitive," Sensei said as I gazed.

"No, no," I said, not wanting to insult it. Already the instrument had ears.

Why I expected anything, I don't know. But the usual markers of beauty—symmetry, balance, a kind of smoothness or sameness—were not here. The instrument was not unlike Sensei herself, a beauty less natural than constructed.

She fluttered onto a stool, reached for the instrument by what appeared to be its throat, and settled it onto her lap. It took several attempts to get it where she wanted it. Playing the shamisen, I soon learned, was not about making it come to you. The shamisen was alive in this way, and required all kinds of careful tending. I wouldn't guess this from looking at it. That day it looked like something easily tamed, a child's toy. Primitive was exactly the word for it.

Then she began to prepare its fragile tuning, turning in small increments its ivory pegs and striking a string, back and forth, until it satisfied. "Would you like to hear a short piece?" she asked, and it seemed for a moment that it was she who was auditioning for lessons.

She played with her eyes to the floor, her hand moving up and down the neck, the sleeve of her kimono fluttering.

Music filled the room, sad and forceful and leaning, as a kind of breeze, colder here, warmer there, but without firm shape. Her pick slapped the skin, her left fingers pinched the strings, and sliding over the notes came her voice in a kind of pained bleating. She made quiet vocal cues when she wasn't singing. She seemed less to be playing the instrument than having a conversation with it.

The sounds fell on my arms like a shawl, sometimes enclosing me, sometimes exposing me. But I was enveloped totally the whole time. If I had tried to stand during that two-minute interval, I don't believe I could have. Something in the music pinned me down, jolted me awake, as if asking me a question.

Then she put a shamisen in my lap and did things that I assumed I should do, too. The more carefully I watched, the more carefully I did them.

On breaks, she brought more tea. How long would I stay in Japan? Were my weekends free? She told me about an American professor, one of few in the world who knew this music. Can you imagine? We can do many things.

I had so many questions—Where did they get the cat skins that covered the sound box? Why was the pick so heavy? Should my nail be splitting like that?—but they seemed childish and jittery in the sober atmosphere of the room, with its charged melancholy music. And I was thrilled to have a future implied, that we would be attached in some way, our destinies thrown together.

Mostly I didn't want to disturb the feeling that with an instrument in my hands, I felt in control again, no longer without aim. There was hope.

=

The music itself was vexing, with the *ma*, and the hard-to-find notes, and the discomfort of merely holding the instrument in my lap. But it stirred my desire, which stirred my ambition.

And longing. I recognized the reverberant, sad, solitary sounds immediately as the same ones that followed me through the streets of Odawara. On these tours I felt solitary but not alone. All around me the Japanese people were sorting themselves into patterns and groups. Something unformed inside me rose up alongside them, like when playing piano as a girl the notes on the staff contained the promise of organizing myself into something useful.

To learn, Sensei said, *"Narau yori nareru.* Do you know this expression?"

I was quite peeved by then. To be struggling in front of her masterful strokes was humiliating. I'd never done anything I couldn't do well right away. Which is probably why things never lasted long, or could hold my interest.

"Instead of learning, Janet, experience."

As it neared noon, Sensei asked if I would like to share a "poor meal." I accepted and followed her into the kitchen. This is how it was: she drifted and I followed. There at the little fold-out table on wheels she explained over bowls of rice and miso soup that the shamisen and voice played in two separate strands that were to never meet. It was the style of the music and it was hard to master. But separate they should stay.

She also laid out the anomaly that the shamisen had become in Japan, stray and unsounded, and in need of hands to play it.

"Do you know how much shamisen lesson cost? 10,000 yen, fifteen minute. How can you learn?"

Along these lines she continued as I perused the little plates she put before me. Rice and bamboo shoots. Miso soup with radish. A plate of pink pickles. I grazed and listened, nodding as she spoke in her unusual English. Unusual not in the way of the phrases I saw on tee shirts and shopping bags: *Level up!* Or, *I want a dream with you!* Sensei's English was unusual in that it said so much with so little, like the shamisen itself: a few notes surrounded by nothing at all.

Brief, clipped, heavily accented, her words always remind me of fat brush strokes on an ink painting with lots of white space around to make them bolder, with the weight of truth. If she was fluent— and I cannot say that she was or was not; as on the shamisen I often wondered, how much did she know?—she was fluent in her own way. She found the words she needed to express what she wanted. And it was something quite urgent. They were the words of a drowning woman, you might say. Words set out like ropes to be taken up by the right people, the ones who understood and had a similar urgent need.

In the kitchen, Sensei put on a checkered smock with keys that jangled in the pocket and contained the sleeves of her kimono. She was as confident here as in the music room. Her kitchen music, I have come to think of it: the whoosh of the refrigerator door; the tick-tick of the gas flame; the kettle that never whistled, only rustled, like wind-blown leaves.

As we ate she shared a brief resume of her life. There was a husband who gambled and drank and stole, to whom she bore two daughters in the same year. Then she threw him out. When the girls were grown, she threw them out, too. "I need my own life," she said.

It was these asides to the music that made me want to sit back, as if in a darkened theater, and watch.

She got up to cut a pear for dessert, fanning the slices on a gold-edged plate. When not speaking, she looked melancholy, and her brightness faded like the strum of a shamisen: a snap dissolving into sadness.

She returned to the table with the plate of fruit. "I want to expand shamisen music more." She rolled a hand near her chest, as if drawing something out. "Foreigners love this music. They can learn. They have passion." She plucked a pink pickle and popped it into her mouth.

How could she be so sure? I wondered. But it intrigued me that she'd thought long and hard about something and become entirely clear on the matter. At the time, there was little I didn't doubt. I had been asking myself since leaving college—the last of the organized places I would exist, when I had music, too, organized on those staves, the notes in their places—what was I to do now? Ordinary life looked bleak and routine, and so I'd reacted with big international gestures.

"I don't like Japanese way," she said. "I think music is about spirit. You are musician. I can tell."

"Not really, I mean, not professional or anything."

She nodded and chewed for a moment.

"What is your purpose, Janet?"

She turned her inky eyes to me. They were very soft kind eyes, and this always surprised me within the framework of her severely cut hair. Inky and slick, like river stones.

As I began to reply with all the reasons why I was in Japan, something had already fallen away. I knew by then, as the sun rose overhead and noon passed—I had been there since early morning— by the way she used her words, by her urgency in teaching me the shamisen, by the kimono and the wild improbable cape of her hair, by the photo she took as I fumbled with a shamisen in my lap— "evidence," she said, though of what I did not know—that this question was not what it seemed.

"I don't want ordinary life," she continued. "Watching TV, going out spend money, seeing friend. *Genki* ...?" she said, imitating the fetching mewl of young Japanese women. "Like your students. I need some purpose."

"*Paaaa-paaaase* ...,*" she said in her thick accent.

We were in something together now. She, me, and the music.

≡

Things started spilling out of me. I laid them on her table along with the plates of pink pickles, waving my chopsticks over the miso bowl, putting my middle finger onto the second stick as I'd seen her do for an easier grip. I went from bowl to bowl, dish to dish, devouring.

I was from a small town, born of working parents who were not familiar with the arts. The exception to this was an aunt, my mother's sister, who took me to concerts, plays, and poetry readings. She gifted me with sacks of books at Christmas, and dropped off videos of Maria Callas or an Ibsen play. We never spoke of them. Nor did my parents.

By her front door, my aunt kept a large sea shell, a footed conch, its pink belly facing up. "Hold it to your ear and you can hear the ocean," she said. Growing up, I would take the hard spiky shell into my hands every time I entered. The mysterious sounds inside the shell excited me and seemed to echo some raw force I felt inside. Like placing my ear to Bach on the cassette player on Sunday mornings after church, I knew these sounds were not outside myself but were a part of me. There was an invisible world within, just at the edge of the visible world.

Sensei nodded knowingly. "*Ehh* ... They can't understand you." She listened and I spoke, until her kimono and the salted salmon and the bamboo shoots fell away, and we were two women in a kitchen sharing secrets.

≡

During our meal, Sensei asked, "Would you like to perform with us in three weeks? We need a singer."

"What do you mean, perform?" I asked.

"Of course. Without performing, no meaning."

My last performance, in a Junior Miss contest at sixteen, crept into my mind and I tried to push it away. Chopin's "Minute Waltz," the repeated refrains and then the bridge, where everything went blank. I'd gone on in the blankness, refusing to stop, striking keys as if knocking on doors to see what was behind them, until one finally opened and the rest of the song tumbled out. Even the trophy they gave me couldn't erase the humiliation I felt.

Sensei dropped her slippers and slid wordlessly into the empty middle room, filling it quickly with garments she peeled out from long thin drawers in a chest against the wall. Kimono, a long white underrobe—"You need monster size," she said—and a pair of white tabi like the ones she was wearing on her feet.

A whiff of aloeswood rose, bitter and sweet. The accumulation of garments was convincing. That she had such power, or a sense of it, drew me closer, and I latched onto the plan easily. If she thought I could, then I could. Saying things out loud, I was learning, was powerful.

"This works?" she asked, holding out a kimono.

I floated over to her and she began to fasten it around me, her tiny hands cinching and fastening. A handful of ties splashed to the floor. Order was not present, nor needed. Something else was at work now. I would learn about Sensei that in her life and her music, there was a companion to order and control, and a time when it should be taken as seriously: intuition.

She held out a split-toed sock. "Try tabi."

I slid my foot inside the cool white cotton and wiggled my toes. It fit.

2

... less notes and rests than irregularities ...

Sensei often said of her music, "We can never know truth." Was *Kurokami* written in 1842? 1840? Was the empty space one beat, or two? Hers was an oral art, transferred person-to-person slowly over time, and even when the music was finally written down, in the late nineteenth century, one could never be sure. This didn't mean Sensei didn't believe in facts. She just believed knowledge of any kind was better in small doses for the same reason emotions were better kept under wraps: knowledge—like feeling—was powerful, and once acquired, it was impossible to turn back.

Her own facts appeared in fragments at lessons or at the kitchen table—the shadow of a maple leaf on the papered doors of her mother's den; the hairstyles of old women in the town she grew up in—each detail enlarging or shifting with metaphoric resonance. It may be I who enlarge, shift, diminish. Our art, and our relationship, is written only now, in an effort to pin down, cohere, make a narrative of all the broken bits, seal once and for all, the empty space of *ma*.

I remember every performance with Sensei, every venue, every stage, even now after twenty years. But how to pinpoint what I learned? It is this that fails me, that lures me into floating in definition. Was it at that first lesson that she told me geisha trained by singing outside in winter to break their voices? That her eldest daughter was a fortune teller? That using the very tip of the finger was best, not the fleshy pad? Her lessons were more like listenings. She seemed less to be teaching me than stirring me round and round, as if distilling me into some ancient wine. The performances were the shape of our days, our years together, but what truly formed us had no time or location or date.

≡

Sensei, if my calculations are right, began her new life teaching foreigners in music at the age of forty-eight. When I met her I think she was fifty-two. She was secretive about her age, like her hair color. If she was forty-eight, it would have been her zodiacal year, the year of the rooster. A preening bird possessive of its hens. It is not an auspicious time. When it is your year, you must be on alert and careful in everything you do or say, so as not to offend the gods.

That year Sensei gave up studying Russian for English.

"Those wars are so passé," said her eldest daughter, the fortune teller I'd once spied in a green kimono hurrying to the station at dusk. "Probably Shinjuku Station tonight," Sensei said, nodding.

Sensei began attending English lessons after work at Trendy House, an English school tucked away in a bank of shops near Shibuya Station. By the time I met her, the school was embroiled in scandal. Embezzling, cooked books, illicit affairs. Sensei's youngest daughter, a graphic designer, would soon produce an acerbic mockumentary about the school called "Let's Do Talk." She wanted Sensei to play the role of the class nerd who keeps calling people out on stuff, the sole moral compass in a sea of vice.

I'm not surprised Sensei hated the classes filled with businessmen, office ladies, and housewives. To abide the mundane dialogues, like the ones I taught in class, must have been a kind of torture on her ears. I can see the sullen lips, the slightly rising chin, the dark boil. It's not that she wasn't humble. In all the time I knew her, Sensei worked at a hospital sterilizing instruments for surgery, a job perhaps only a step above making tea for executives. I tried to picture her in scrubs and long yellow gloves at a basin of shiny steel scalpels. She kept a long pair of bandage shears in a drawer in the music room, her "revenge" dagger, she joked, for students who didn't practice. She would never think of leaving her day job. To her, it was security for her life in music.

Soon she engaged a private teacher from Australia, Jacqueline. Through Jacqueline she learned that foreigners wanted to know more about "the real Japan." They sought out old things they could touch and feel and take home with them. What space opened in Sensei hearing this? What new thoughts? What new way of being amid direct words, broad gestures, laughter, freshness?

Was it plan or coincidence that she had a shamisen with her one day at a lesson? She would have settled it on Jacqueline's lap at the thirty-degree angle, placed the heavy oak pick in her hand, and showed her the protective strike zone on the cat skin below. She would have called out numbers and corrected her for *ma*, the little sips of silence between the notes. Showed her how to use *hito-sashiyubi*, "the pointing-at-other-people finger," sliding it along the strings until the nail split and a small callous began to form on its tip.

Jacqueline came to her house on weekends for lessons. Sensei did not believe in charging money for something that should be about "pure spirit," so her lessons were free. The day job, giving free lessons to foreigners—this was how she kept herself apart from the traditional world and is part of the complicated legacy from which she comes.

Sensei left her hometown of Toyama City at eighteen and never looked back. Her mother's family had considerable wealth but lost everything in the fire bombings, which destroyed the whole city. Her mother was a dancer in the Nishikawa guild who, at twenty-three, had met Sensei's father, a besotted sixteen-year-old who helped with her performances.

"Terrible match," Sensei said. Her father became a high school principal. Her mother kept dancing.

Sensei was born at the end of the war. Her given name meant "sincerity" and was a man's name in Japan, but I've been told that after Japan's defeat, in the postwar democracy, under an American constitution, it was a popular name to maintain the old Japanese spirit as the nation entered a new age.

The traditional arts must have felt unfashionable to a young woman growing up in the 1950s. Dance with her mother, an incursion on her own dreams. She went out after school with boys, smoking cigarettes in her kimono. I can imagine the erotic allure of that. She loved Pat Boone, long walks in the mountains, and when she was eighteen, she went to Tokyo to find her own music.

Being from Toyama, a small city on the Sea of Japan, she must have felt like a hick. She stayed with her sister and brother-in-law until her mother could find her a teacher at the Fine Arts University. She was looking for a teacher of *nagauta*, the "long songs" of her own dances. There was no other choice. One didn't dabble or explore freely. Music was taught, like long plaits of hair, in direct lineages, passed on in guilds by powerful patriarchs.

I suspect that Sensei already played the shamisen, that her mother taught her so she could play for her dance students. If so, she knew this music, its tempos: less notes and rests than irregularities, like sound and its interruption. Beforeness and afterness.

Finding Kikuoka-sensei changed her world forever and set her apart, as he himself did, and gave her a model for going it alone, for being a maverick. Though their musical lives couldn't have been more different, inside, I think, it gave her strength, this identification with his spirit.

Kikuoka-sensei was handsome, silver-haired, fatherly, with a big smile. On stage, he sat in the center of the long back row, as unmoving as a potted plant, his skill visible only in his surefooted strumming, and an almost supernatural sense of the singer's timing beside him. As he played the shamisen, he entered the music so fully that he seemed to have disappeared, fusing with the three strings, the long heavy neck. The effect of this on me whenever I saw him play was vivid. Sensei's teacher's playing always made me feel, if not that I could play quite like that, that it was worth doing.

His idea was to build a musical group based on skill and merit and not patronage of musical heads of state. Players would use their own names, be listed in the program as themselves instead of following custom and taking on the patriarch's last name. The group was called To-on-kai, short for Tokyo Ongaku Kai, the Tokyo Music Society. Every season their small quarterly program, a robin's egg blue with simple black characters, appeared clipped to Sensei's calendar.

"You don't have the heart for this," Kikuoka-sensei told her one day and advised her to remain an amateur. I wonder if he saw how she darkened at the slights and barbs of competing students, how she complained of unfairness, her hurt and anger. If he saw that and wanted to save her the heartache, and save the music for her, too.

During the difficult years after her divorce, he waived her lesson fees and let her barter for work in the house with his wife, a retired dancer. She stirred the *kinton*, chewy chestnut sweet, over the stove for days at New Year's and massaged his wife's shoulders. She sold tickets to his concerts. When she asked how she could pay him back, he told her, "Teach."

But here was the interruption. Unable to take his name in the usual way of family clans, nor wanting to enter the professional world she couldn't bear to join, she was alone with her music.

Her marriage did not define her, nor her daughters, nor her mother. She would go on until she found Jacqueline. After Jacqueline there was Gerry, a Canadian, who left her to learn folk music. Every year, during cherry blossom season, when the petals were lining the streets of Tokyo like pink frosting, Sensei would turn to the window. "Gerry must be near Sendai now," where the northern cherries were in bloom and there was money to be made busking.

It was Gerry who found the American professor's papers. Sensei wrote a letter, telling the professor of her idea to teach foreigners. She did not charge because music should be free. She would shame the Japanese, into doing what or how, I never learned.

"Why not teach Japanese?" I asked her that first day. "That way they can pass it on."

She stared at me as if I were a small child. "Complicated," she said. "You will see." Something went dark when she said this, and the atmosphere changed, like we were in one of those snow globes, enclosed in something you can never get out of.

Then she brightened. "Anyway, we should enjoy." She raised her chin and sipped her tea, folding the edge of her bob at her jawline.

I later found out she'd been born with waves. It was a rainy day and we were in formal attire, heading to a concert, and she was panicking about the weather. She ran back into her rooms and emerged wearing a green silk scarf tied on her head, and when I asked, she admitted that her hair was wavy. She seemed relieved to have caught it in time, to prevent what was natural from coming out, keeping the waves straight and drawn evenly to an icy line at her neck.

3

… an ongoing conversation between the living and the dead …

I once stayed at a Zen temple where it was forbidden at meals to pick up a dish with one hand. The slight adjustment was profound. With no chance for preoccupation with the other hand, no grabbing lightly while lost in thought, I was brought more fully into what I was doing. It made the act devotional, which could perhaps be defined, for lack of better words, as doing something "with both hands."

In those first days after meeting Sensei I began to live in Japan "with both hands."

I still sat on the bed in the mornings, sipping my ritual cup of Nescafé while staring out at the waves of Sagami Bay. I walked to school with Larry, up the hill, past the cemetery, to our campus near a tea farm. But now I met the eyes of women on balconies trimming bonsai or hanging laundry, who called out, *"Itterasshai!"* the ritual leave-taking phrase, "Please go and come back safely," and answered, *"Ittekimasu!"* "I will go now and return."

I started taking my students to dinner in Chinatown, or little pubs where I could pester them about Japanese music. I promised Larry no baseball or bowling outings. We sat at these gatherings, surrounded by a pod of students asking, Did I own a gun? What was my favorite movie?

None had seen a shamisen, but they told me what they knew. The sitting position, on the knees, would be painful. It meant discipline and hard study. And then they offered words like *gaman* (staying power), and *seishin* (spirit). They wished me luck. *Ganbatte!* They were happy I liked Japan. One girl pulled me aside. I will never forget Etsuko, tall and willowy, with slanted eyeteeth and a glamour somehow despite them. She'd once told me her skin was yellow because of a problematic "river." Etsuko threw her hair over one shoulder and said the traditional arts were wife training. "Japanese wife needs to learn obedience and duty." Etsuko and the other girls were looking for husbands with the three "highs": tall, high salary, the high nose of a foreigner.

I wove shamisen into conversations with school personnel and 7-Eleven clerks. "*Erai!*" strangers said, akin to "Good girl!" or "*Omoshiroi ...*" a word that meant both "interesting" and "funny."

I went looking for a book on Japanese music. Not because I didn't trust Sensei, though the whole situation was so unreal, so unexpected, that I had to wonder. Why would she teach music to foreigners who would soon leave? Were there really no scales, no ways to practice or warm up?

I took a crowded elevator up to the fifth floor of English books at the Kinokuniya store. In the spot on the shelf where the professor's book on Japanese music would be was a blank. It was out of print, said a salesgirl. I wandered into a nearby department store and followed the signs for musical instruments. Shamisen were displayed on glass shelves under spotlights, their necks long and glossy. A salesgirl showed how it came apart in three pieces and was easy to carry home in a suitcase on an airplane. I shook my head and wandered into stationery, where I bought a black leather *techo*, appointment book, that fit in the palm of my hand and came wrapped in a box like a Christmas present. In the square for October 16, 1996, I wrote with the attached pen, "Concert in Kamakura" and looked at it from time to time, a place in the sea of blank pages where I was expected to be.

"Performance brings out peoples' personalities," Sensei said when she called with updates. I listened, absorbed into her concerns about food, clothing, people, transportation. Who was a vegetarian? How many kimono dressers did we need? And most of all the weather. "Out of my control," she said mournfully, and spoke of autumn typhoons that could race up the coast and deluge us and our instruments.

Larry was there on the periphery of it all, quiet, easygoing, preparing his lessons and coming in from his reading to the spare bedroom where I'd set up to practice singing. Despite my pleas that I couldn't sing, Sensei had handed me a cassette tape on my way out the door. *Ame no Goro*, "Goro's Rain," was composed in 1841 and retold the medieval legend of two samurai, the Soga brothers, who avenge their father's death. In the accompanying translation, I saw a lot of "drenched dew" and "knotweed."

"Sounds more like a love story," I said.

Sensei sighed. "It's always a love story."

"What's that noise?" Larry said when he came in. "Sounds like someone's been stuck by a cattle prod."

"It's Goro," I explained. "These are his last moments before ritual suicide. You'd be sad, too."

"Oh," he said and left.

If the sudden and unexpected connection to everything around me felt like a door was opening, it was the return to the music that pulled me inside. I had forgotten what it was like to be in a piece of music, going back and forth over it, honing, polishing. It was like a limb had been missing and resprouted anew.

When Larry left, I laid out the score at my knees. To say that I could not sing the song is too simple. What sounded easy was extremely difficult to imitate. As on the shamisen, I was focused on the notes rather than the spaces between. And the notes didn't seem to be notes. Not like notes I knew, that sat on a staff and didn't move, that had a value and a shape, a place, up or down, high or low, sharp or flat.

All I can say is that the notes of the Japanese voices on my tape seemed to contain all these qualities at once. As soon as they began, they seemed to move, away from their origin and toward their destination but in no straight line I could hear. They seemed to ascend while descending, stop while continuing. I can think of no other way to put it, only to say that it was very complicated. And seemed completely possible until I tried to do it.

I rewound, listened again. I broke a page down into a line, a measure, a beat, a breath, straining to distinguish the most imperceptible differences. Soon exhausted, I would give up and roll off my knees.

And yet the tune was infectious. It followed me everywhere. On my steps up the hill to school, making tea in my room. If I'd been listening and then gone out walking, I heard the notes in the sound of a shoe on the stairs, a murmur in a shop, the trickle of water, a bird's cry. The result of my utter failure to produce the note, I see now, was the beginning of listening intensely.

Sensei told me not to worry.

"But I don't know where the music's going. It seems to just do what it wants." I wrote a Western staff in an attempt to place the notes. But even with that, using the only language I could use to describe what I was hearing, I failed. It was like I had the wrong ears to hear it.

And the overall quality of the voices and singing style was impossible to render. Where Western voices sail clear to high C, and treasure clarity and polish, all I can say is these voices sounded broken, tortured, as they revved in the throat and bleated like a raw wind over the sea.

Each time Sensei called with updates on concert preparations, I expected her to reveal some key piece of information that would unlock the technique, but none came. I hoped to learn more when I returned to her rooms the next Saturday for another lesson.

It was only a week later, but autumn had arrived. The skies were clear and the air freed from summer's clutches. I followed the route she had shown me, down the busy road, Kannana-dori, which I named that day "Lucky Seven," passing the barber shop and the car dealership, where Ichiro in his Giants uniform was still smiling on a flag. At the cherry tree at the entrance of her housing complex, I turned in and headed up the three stairs and down the concrete veranda.

Outside the steel door to #105, I heard two shamisen snapping crisply. The door rattled when I knocked.

"*Hai, dozo!*" Sensei yelled, not stopping her teaching.

"You have to wait," she said to the tall foreign woman on the stool as I slipped off my loafers and stepped up into the kitchen.

"Space!"

The woman was Denise, a six-foot bashful blonde from Georgia. You'd never know she was about to dance as Goro in the show. She chose male dances instead of female, because of her height, but I suspect she preferred flashing muscle and downing cups of sake to permissive mincing and gazing at the moon.

"I'm a bull in a China shop around here," she sighed.

Her dance school was the same as Sensei's mother.

"All connected," Sensei beamed.

"She's a national treasure," Denise told me later. She only came to learn shamisen to be around her.

Soon arriving were Lisa, an exchange student at Waseda, and a tall man Sensei called Douggie, who handed her a box of Hershey's ice cream pops that she tucked into the freezer. Most of her students were Americans.

Over tea and rice crackers, they talked about another student, The Enchanting Creature, who apparently had gone missing. Then it was time to rehearse.

In the music room, Sensei, Doug, Lisa, and I kneeled on a line of cushions, while Denise struck a pose in the empty middle room. Sensei cued a tape and the music began, somber, rigidly organized, and baffling. Next to me Doug plucked a shamisen. Lisa tapped a hand drum next to Sensei, who was playing a small round drum with two long sticks. It was hard to hear the taped music over all the instruments and Denise stomping under her umbrella. My urge to understand pressed on me. I blurted out notes, trying not to sing in the blank spaces.

At the end of the song, Sensei kneeled beside me. "You can sing kind of quietly, how do you say, lip synch, it's OK. Most important is to look professional."

As in the shamisen lesson, my concern was with the note. That is what would either embarrass me or not. It was the one thing I had control over, I thought. But it was what fell around the note that was important, like the form of the singer as she sat and fulfilled her role. This was about not embarrassing others.

A form, or *kata*, is a precise exercise, a foundational stroke. "*Kata* is a boundary or skin," my journals say, "where the individual heart meets collective experience." *Kata* are what allow a beginner to go onstage, to join the flow, providing safe harbor in unknown seas. The *kata* sets you up for a lifetime of artistic practice. A *kata* was reliable.

While the others took a tea break and stretched their legs, Sensei demonstrated.

I took some issue at first with being shown how to sit and turn a page. But it soon became clear. I was moving too much: bending, reaching, turning. I had to do one thing after another. Linear, slow, literal.

When it came time to sing, I was to pick up a tiny fan Sensei set by my knees. The fan was never to be opened. I should find it with my fingers not my eyes, and when contacting the smooth bamboo rib under my thumb, draw it gently up into my lap where my left palm should lay open to receive it.

We tried again and the music unspooled like a heavy wave, rising and falling around us. Reach but not move. Find but not look.

This was the beginning of the great funneling, the whittling of impulses into a first form. Here, without the basic vocal training or ability to even follow or hear exactly where the notes were going, I was pruning and taming the body into a recognizable shape in the world. A *kata* was doable, even if the music was not. It hallowed my actions, giving something trivial great weight and importance.

Getting inside things without words. Infection without understanding.

I have often wondered why Sensei invited me to perform when I knew so little. Did she see a talented person who might be useful to her mission? Or a girl full of desire who needed a form to realize those desires in the world?

Embodying a *kata* meant being recognizable in her world, and in Japan. With effort and time, you could polish, along with the actions, your true intention.

"How much do we know reality?" she said one day years later at a diner in Vermont where she'd come to visit. Among the plates of lasagna, scalloped potatoes, and apple pie, she said, "This is reality, but in a way, just food. We are anxious every day. What is normal way? We are looking, but it doesn't exist. That's why, curiosity and desire are a necessity."

Instead of duty, she meant. If one is to find one's own true path, one has to bear desire. Be able to contain the dream.

=

After rehearsal we were whisked off to the theater. Sensei had ordered us tickets for a one-curtain show. The woman had plans. This was not meant to be entertainment but *benkyo*, study. Kabuki theater was the historical genesis of Sensei's music.

The dance was *Musume Dojoji*, "The Maiden at Dojo Temple," Sensei explained on the train, leaning over her tote bag brimming with music scores and snacks, hands clasped, as if delivering a lecture or blessing.

A woman has fallen in love with a priest. When he spurns her, she comes to his temple, pretending to be collecting subscriptions, and traps him under the temple bell and turns into a snake ghost. "Women are demons," Sensei said, wiggling two index fingers by her ears.

Denise jumped in with the story of Okuni, the shrine maiden who invented kabuki in the sixteenth century but whose shows had, apparently, been shut down for lewdness. Now men acted women's roles onstage.

"Women can't play on stage at the kabuki," Denise said. "No matter how good they are."

"Such a feudal society. That's why I don't like," Sensei said.

Today's show would be danced by an *onnagata*, a female impersonator.

"*Hengemono*," Sensei instructed, as we settled into front-row seats in the balcony. A female transformation play. "Most popular."

We had opted not to buy earphone guides. We were there for the music anyway. Sensei passed out cream puffs and tea and looked around. A smattering of foreigners and Japanese sat in the balcony. Below us were three floors of seats, the first of which hugged a raised walkway that cut through the audience at stage right. This was the *hanamichi*, "flower path," Denise said, for dramatic exits and entrances.

Sensei scanned the stage with binoculars as the curtain rose. There were two, a heavy formal one that rose automatically, and underneath a thinner one pulled open by stage hands.

"Lead singer is my sensei's favorite," she whispered. "And the drummer?" She indicated a silver-maned man whose drum ropes were violet, not orange, like the others. "Very womanizer."

The musicians were kneeling on a vermilion carpet in two tiered rows at the side of the stage. I counted eighteen in all: shamisen players, drummers, a flute player, and singers who had the little fan closed at their knees and were the only ones with music stands reading a score. There was no conductor. All musicians faced front, unmoving. A shamisen began a slow tattoo, and a singer released a throaty howl. The spareness—the spookiness—cast a hush and we, too, stopped moving to listen.

Soon we heard the screeching of curtain hooks and a collective gasp as heads turned to look. Applause rose like a wave, and finally, creeping into our view, on the *hanamichi*, was the dancer, white-faced, in a flat red hat, dipping and swooning her way to the stage. She (he?) took her time, advancing, retreating, letting her long ornately stitched kimono tease over the edge. "For his patrons," Sensei said later.

The theater remained in half-light, the color of late afternoon. People ate lunchboxes and drank small cans of tea. They stepped out and returned. The box seats were lined with ladies in kimono, and a few men, too. It all had a festive feel, like an extended picnic.

Every so often, a male voice from the rear shouted, "*Matte imashita!*" "I was waiting for that!" Or "*Yamatoya!*" (an actor's guild name). These people were plants, Sensei said. People today did not know the plays well enough to play this role anymore. For kabuki was a collaboration between the audience and the actors, who traversed the space between them, eclipsing it, and expanding it, in dizzying spontaneous howls. In this way tradition was alive: an ongoing conversation between the living and the dead.

From time to time Sensei's hands rose to her lap and tapped out drumbeats. I could feel the force of her concentration as her small hands pat-pat-patted, sometimes crossing each other and landing noiselessly in her lap. I think that's when it began to hit me that Sensei was composing a life in this music. It was her personal choice. Her day job only gave her the freedom to love it all the more, to devote herself to it without question.

It took time. There was no substitute when everything was learned—"stolen"—through exposure to the art in discreet moments of witnessing or observation. The most important thing you could do, then, was to show up, to prepare yourself for learning. Even my codified gestures—legs folded, eyes down—were setting up a kind of condition so that something might sink in.

At one point, the dancer paused and knelt in the middle of the stage, her long sleeves crossed on her lap like a butterfly's wings.

Sensei whispered, "*Hikinuki,* special technique …"

A man dressed in black scurried onto the stage and disappeared behind the dancer. The shamisen entered a drone, the singing stopped. The man was moving, arms flying quickly, and then everything stopped and the dancer burst forward, as from a cocoon, her shed layer in the hands of the man now ferrying it off stage.

The risk of such a trick made me dizzy. I swooned at everything that could have gone wrong but didn't. I was still swooning as the dancer mounted the bell in the last scene, in a silver kimono patterned with triangular "scales," waving a demon's trident, her white face leering at us as the curtain was pulled across the stage.

The image remained with me as we filed down the stairs with the crowds of people and stood out front to take a picture. A drum boomed and a festival flute trilled. Women in kimono were rushing to find taxis. I felt like everything was moving and nothing was moving at all, like the dance, a series of stops and starts of still life tableaux. Mostly, I didn't want to leave the theater. I had an inexplicable longing to go back in and see it all again, to maybe never leave, as I watched Denise line us up in the viewfinder.

Sensei stood behind me, one step up, in pedal pushers and a raincoat cinched at her waist. I leaned forward on my umbrella in an Edwardian blazer, giddy. In yellow-lit windows above, I imagined the actors rubbing greasepaint from their cheeks, maybe sipping a whiskey. They would be in cotton robes and soon they would leave the theater for dinner, or home, for tomorrow they would return to do it again. Somewhere up there, too, was an old man with a needle and thread, who would stay late into the night to sew those kimono back together, stitch by stitch, until all the layers were invisible.

"*Hai cheezu!*" yelled Denise.

And then, somewhere between Denise's signal to pose and the click of the flash, Sensei did something I would never have expected her to do, knowing as I did, something of Japanese life. I had visited families for maple-viewing or hot-pot suppers and found them absent of pats on the hand or kisses on the cheek, any touching, in other words, or evidence of affection.

And yet that is what she did. As the shutter clicked and the crowds found their way to trains or bars, Sensei placed her hand on my right shoulder.

How to describe the significance of this? The gesture, so small but so radical. It is hard to convey. I continue to study the picture, to see again what she meant for me. Was she claiming? Anointing? Letting me know that she wanted Western familiarity, not Japanese?

Sensei never wanted to be called a teacher, literally "the one who came before." But that is what she was, if learning in Japan was an intimacy with strangers, those people you would never meet or know, who had, long before you, created the forms, the gestures, the *kata*, that you would fill. Everyone had a role, even the man in black, a propsman coming to the aid of the actor. It wasn't important what the role was, but having a role at all.

Perhaps, this, too, was my *benkyo*, and what her hand meant to say.

4

… her tabi looked ecstatically shabby …

The reason Japanese students are pushed to perform too early, it has struck me, is to experience helplessness and panic. Only then, pinned in fear and shame, is the *kata* tattooed on the heart.

It is one theory anyway, and it was like this for me. Held in place by the starched silk sash pressing at my ribs and restricting me to only shallow sips of breath, I made sounds on stage that day too soft for anyone to hear. I felt small, swallowed up. But the music was holding me in place, as were the memories of the kabuki cream puffs, the rehearsal at Sensei's, the practice tape, the sea, and Larry, all infused with the voices and shamisen, darting and diving. I was part of something already.

Hours before settling on my knees on the vermilion carpet, before my calves began their prickly descent into sleep, we were breakfasting at Mister Donut. Sensei wore a handkerchief in her obi as a bib and craned her neck over a bowl of egg drop soup. Savory dumplings and egg rolls were available alongside the glazed donuts and powdery crullers that Denise, Douggie, Lisa, and I ordered.

Sensei had meticulously mapped out our route to the Kamakura Performing Arts Center. She might even have taken the route herself in advance. She was known to do things like this, planning every last thing in her control before going onstage where, everyone knew, you couldn't predict what would happen.

The morning had brought a low-grade earthquake followed by

clear skies and unseasonably high temperatures. Denise was convinced the natural event was a blessing from Goro's spirit.

"Goro existed when Kamakura was the capital of Japan, in the twelfth century," she explained on the way to the train.

"Shogun was Yoritomo," Sensei said. "Very bad guy."

On the fifteenth floor of the Kamakura Performing Arts Center, we stepped off the elevator into a kind of controlled chaos. Fake spears and wisteria branches were making their way on the shoulders of propsmen to an area behind the curtains, where they'd be taken up by a dancer or stagehand. Girls were carrying trays of tea to green rooms laid with sweet-smelling tatami, and female musicians roosted in circles talking and swapping stories, their hair sprayed into French twists cinched with glamorous combs. Men roamed the halls smoking, shuffling in their slippers, or stood in corners together, nodding and puffing.

"God," Lisa said, "when Japanese men are attractive, they *really* are."

They looked like samurai in their black silk kimono and formal *hakama* skirts. Black was the color of the day, casting a funereal gloom. "The uniform," Sensei called the black robe with the family crest, plain but for the hemline on female robes, which were splashed with gold-stitched patterns of cherry, crane, bamboo.

Sensei insisted that "joining" was the point of coming, not singing. Perhaps this is where she thought she could woo me best, in the exclusive backstage arena. It would have been smart of her. The enticements were almost more than I could bear. The patterns, the hair combs, the sounds of musicians tuning their instruments: a cicada-like buzz of the shamisen, the dry *tik* of an *okawa*, the watery *pom* of a *tsuzumi*, the ringing strike of a *taiko*. Sensei identified these sounds and more.

At breakfast she'd noticed that I'd rimmed my eyes in kohl.

"You put on make?" she asked.

I nodded, embarrassed, not only for my vanity—someone more self-assured would not need to paint themselves up—but because it seemed to imply that what she was giving me was not enough, I'd needed to add something more.

"Very beautiful," she said and returned to her soup.

Backstge, Doug went to the men's dressing area, Denise headed for costumes, and Lisa and I followed Sensei to a gymnasium laid with straw mats on another floor, where we were dressed in borrowed robes. Mine had no pattern, which didn't matter because I would be on my knees, where any ornamentation would be hidden. It was in fact a funeral robe, which must have confused the woman dressing me since she crossed my lapels right over left, the forbidden pattern reserved only for dressing a corpse. I waved Sensei over and she whispered to the woman, who parted the robe quickly and began again, apologizing profusely.

Sensei looked natural in kimono, and minced along like a girl from the past, as if she were not at all encumbered by the ties or clips at her ribs, the wraparound skirt, the dangling sleeves. She knew how to move in one, in other words, whereas I had to learn to hold sleeves away from door handles. The folds under the sash bunched up because of my hips and needed smoothing. My collar yawned.

This was her world, in other words, a place where she belonged and I did not, even as she drew out a boxwood comb and, drawing it along her oiled strands, said of the women, "Dragon ladies. So fake. This has nothing to do with music."

Whether it was the kimono or her barbs, I felt raised up, taller, more feminine and more powerful in my robe. I greeted each master she brought me to like approaching the communion wafer at church: eyes trained low, the syllables forming like waves on my tongue.

Yoroshiku onegai shimasu. Please forgive me for any errors I will make today or am making right now.

I bowed, showing them the top of my head. The robe was dictating my movements now, mincing my steps, tucking my elbows. I enjoyed the way the silk fluttered as I walked, the way I could hide things in my obi or sleeves.

It is shocking to me now that she was allowed to go where she went, to glide from foreigners to seasoned masters, from intruders to insiders, and no one said a word. She was allowed, on the surface anyway, to go wherever she needed to go. Was this her intent, too? To show me her power?

She always spoke in English. When we had a spare moment she taught me how to fold a kimono, lining up the seams, and executing a series of folds until it was the size of a shoebox.

Doug reappeared and was making small talk in Japanese when Sensei stopped him. She reached into her obi for a handkerchief and led him to a water fountain, where she dabbed at a driblet of chocolate drying on the collar of his pale blue borrowed silk kimono. Doug apologized profusely.

"I will have to dry clean," she said as we walked away. "Very expensive."

That day, Sensei was showing her mastery not just of the music or her mission to teach it the way she believed it should be taught, but of her ability to traverse two worlds: one she hated but was stuck with, and the one she chose and loved.

=

I saw more and more why Sensei might want to avoid all the complications I was seeing around me, fascinated though I was. Professionals were groomed to embody the forms and pass them on strictly because of birth. Anyone wanting in had to pay, in money and in loyalty, which, with any luck, would end up in adoption into the clan. Everyone else remained an amateur.

It was from amateurs' wallets that the money flowed, in slim tidy envelopes stuffed with brand new bills no one had touched yet except the clerk at the bank, who ran it through a machine and then fanned it like a hand of cards to count it in front of you. Bills for stagehands, musicians, propsmen, wig makers, makeup artists, and costumers. People bringing extra strings or a heater to toast the skin of the *okawa*. Ticket takers and food bearers and tea servers. The money went upward, to the *iemoto*, grandmasters, some of whom were Living National Treasures.

Denise's fees totaled a few thousand dollars. "Hell, I have no kids. It's my fortieth birthday present to myself."

My envelope contained thirty dollars and a handwritten note to the lead singer. Sensei assured me the note should be written in English.

"But can she read it?"

"More honorable," she said.

Sensei's envelopes contained no notes. For Japanese, the money was the note. This part of the music world was *inshitsu na*, Sensei said, one of the "dark humid places" of Japan where things like bribes, bullying, and pornography lurked.

Through it all Sensei walked, hands clasped, like a monk on morning rounds, stepping this way and that, from one world to another, to anywhere she wanted to go. Her white cotton tabi were 21 cm, a child's size. The toe of one, I noticed, during all the bowing and envelope-passing, was fraying. It was a contrast to the formality of her robe, a mismatch. She was too careful to not know. Why not break out a fresh pair for the occasion?

I have come to see this frayed toe as elemental to her nature. It reminded me of her rooms: worn and fading but buffed and shined daily. Human effort in the face of the inevitable.

The toe of her tabi, in other words, to me, was sheer hope. No matter how worn down, one could still be in the game. It was a refusal to be defeated, a poverty of things, but not of spirit. By the end of the day her tabi looked ecstatically shabby.

=

At 11 a.m. we left the encampment for the stage. Behind the curtain we assembled ourselves into two tiers, the first for drummers and flute, the second containing an equal number of shamisen and singers. I kneeled at the far end of the singers, at stage right, the seat of lowest rank.

Everyone bowed from their knees one last time, apologizing, pleading, excusing, until, finally, we settled in. Sensei was directly below me on her drum.

The curtain peeled open and wooden blocks slapped furiously at the edge of the stage. The audience applauded. And then silence. And then, as if in code, two taps. *Ki! Ki!* A shamisen strummed, a slow cranking up of the song that stirred the lead singer to moan, "*Saruhodo ni* ..." "Well, once upon a time ..." The voice went up and down, all rumble and ride. The shamisen plucked and fired, and ended on a fading ostinato.

Shan! Denise stomped out in her three-inch clogs, wielding her umbrella, wearing an oversized black kimono with butterflies stitched on its skirts, with red leggings and a purple obi sash that looked like twisted balloon art.

I folded my hands on my lap and kept my eyes low.

Bench, reach, do not search but find.

My lips opened.

Was I singing?

Whose sound was whose?

The music moved fast, like a river, past us all. The shamisen toiled, all slap and buzz and stick, embellishing, adding, building hard. Drums ticked and popped below. Sensei's drumsticks appeared to splash the patch of deer skin in the center of her drum. A flute started shredding the air. I let them all fill me, like the bittersweet incense on the sleeve of an old geisha singing next to me, the glint of Sensei's famous hair below.

An infant in Japan is not age zero but one. At birth, the shape is already there, the way known. She does not have to become anything that has not existed already.

I sang so softly I couldn't be sure I was singing. My goal was to be invisible, to prostrate myself, to surrender completely to the musical past. After, I unfolded my legs gingerly. *Ki o tsukete*, everyone was murmuring, Easy does it. My knees ached, my ribs hurt.

But I knew, at least now, the shape of what must be filled.

≡

Later, over a bowl of soba noodles near the station, Sensei asked of my performance, "How did you go?" We had left the concert hall even though the music continued. "Fine, I think. It was hard to tell." I felt slack again in Western clothes. Three weeks, in which had passed a couple of lessons and a kabuki show, in which I hadn't exactly learned to sing, now unspooled and I was back in my life.

We stood in a knot at the turnstile of Ofuna Station, where housewives with bags of groceries were hurrying home and teen-aged girls clutching Tiffany bags were laughing and pointing at shop windows.

A subtle tension in Sensei was now gone. We'd gotten through without major gaffes. Doug's chocolate mishap could be cleaned. My sudden muteness was forgivable. Lisa missed a few drumbeats but we'd be spared. It had all worked out.

Greatly relieved, we all laughed, a little buzzed relief.

I turned to Sensei. Did one hug Sensei? Before I could decide she slipped through the ticket gates, her raspberry lace kimono coat humped over the obi like a little camel. Something was radiating in her that had not been present before the show, some flush of content-ment within. Doug followed, his red nylon shamisen bag like a great oar on his back; Denise, her blond hair twisted into a proud crown; Lisa, blending in with her dark hair and pale skin.

Sensei turned and my heart skipped a beat. Already I had no idea what I would do without her. "Call me next week! I am going to Kyoto in the morning to look for drums."

They receded and I felt like I did in the entryway, or *genkan*, of Japanese homes, no longer a part of the interior, but not yet outside, either.

5

… found not by fret but intuition …

I sometimes think my affair with Japanese music started with a sock, the tabi Sensei slipped onto my foot that first day. Subtly, it emboldened me to revisit something I had no courage to revisit—music, nowhere and then suddenly here, a shamisen, in Japan—and it changed something. After I slipped my foot inside and let its cool cotton encase my foot, everything fell into place. The only way to explain all this is to say that it was as if, after meeting Sensei and performing on stage, I had aged many years.

In class at my school in Odawara, I cracked open the blue curriculum binder and saw the dialogues my students repeated as a fine way to learn a language. Their inability to speak in class or discuss world events ceased to annoy me. During games, where I'd once encouraged them to demolish the competition, I now saw the collective way of helping more fun.

I became more indulgent and parental, like Japanese teachers, nodding my head sympathetically when a girl told me privately that her friend was absent due to period pain. A few months before I would have clucked silently, "Get over it!" but now I considered that, yes, periods were painful and I had often used a hot water bottle to soothe the tender ache.

I developed a taste for leggy enoki mushrooms and pickled plums. I still ate curried noodles in the cafeteria but no longer had to season my white rice with grated cheese, enjoying the pearly grains plain. The change was less a deliberate decision than a natural occurrence, as if something inside me had said, "It's time to eat plain rice now," and so I did.

I dared myself with new foods at the well-stocked 7-Elevens: hot Chinese dumplings stuffed with red bean paste, coffee jelly, and *oden*, a sweet-salty broth in a slotted pot at the counter from which the clerk ladled fish cakes, chicken meatballs, and radish slices fat as hockey pucks.

Once on, you can't take a tabi off again. Your toes remember the new arrangement: one big toe, the four others nestled together, like a tiny hoof. After the concert, everything was about collecting more experiences that aligned with this new shape—the sock, the kimono, the music with its sad sounds and silences. Every experience shot through me, jolting me awake, challenging me to understand but not without first absorbing all I could.

I took Larry to a noh play at Odawara Castle. As with the singing, foisted upon me when I really just wanted to learn the shamisen, the concert was less a plan than a result of circumstance.

I had been admiring a flyer for it in the office at school, and the next day, a young woman, Miyuki, who had come to Kamakura to see my "singing debut," gave me two tickets.

"I couldn't," I said.

"Please," she insisted. "Enjoy Japanese culture."

Noh was older than kabuki, and more sacred. Started in the fourteenth century, noh told stories with Buddhist themes—less stories than prayer-dances—and was the art performed for the shogun. Apparently, the shogun at the time was watching noh when Commodore Perry's Black Ships landed on Japan's shores in 1853 demanding access, interrupting the afternoon.

The castle grounds had been set up with folding chairs and a stage. As the sky darkened, two great torches were lit, throwing shadows onto the pebbly ground. Seats were full, mostly of older people. I waited, leaning forward. Larry sat with the heels of his cowboy boots dug into the earth.

An actor appeared, his white tabi peeking out from under his oversized kimono. A mask hid his face and seemed to float off from his body as he made his way down a ramp to the stage. He was hardly moving, each toe advancing only a couple of inches. Drummers howled, winding up their arms and bringing them down in sharp slaps on their drums. Chanting began, of a chorus to the right and behind the mask in the actor's faraway trapped voice. A flute shrieked, indifferent but insistent.

There was nothing to hold onto. No strings, no singing. Just chanting and the glacial mincing. I leaned in, determined to squeeze some meaning out of the elevated impenetrable art.

I heard snoring. Around me I saw heads lowering, chins bobbing. Larry jerked awake. The torches at the edges of the stage crackled. How could these people fall asleep? At the end of the show, I was bursting with questions.

Larry and I walked up the hill to our apartment, in the opposite direction of the castle. The gas station was closed, the sea beyond, invisible.

"What did you think?" I asked.

"It was like a haiku," he said. "There ain't much there."

"That's it?" I said.

He shrugged.

I rolled over that night, saying I was tired, but wanting to think of what Sensei would say about what I was seeing and doing. Mostly I just wanted to be alone with my new memories: Lucky Seven Boulevard lined with shimmering golden ginkgos, Sensei's simple steel door, the feel of the shamisen's long thin neck, the jangling, almost upsetting sound of its strings. She had suggested I purchase a shamisen—"you need to practice," she said—and had ordered one from Kameya, a family of makers she was loyal to. I wondered if it would look like the ones in her rooms, covered in cat skin, their necks like deep shiny seas.

The next morning, I told Larry, "I can't find my lesson plan. You go ahead. I'll catch up." I waited until I knew he'd be far up the hill, probably running into students by now, and then I headed out, leaving my Sony Walkman behind, feeling my feet on solid ground. At every clink of breakfast dishes or sliding open of *fusuma* doors, my heart leapt. Lines blurred. I was inside with them now too.

≡

Skies cleared and Mount Fuji, that tall white crayon, loomed visibly now on the horizon. Wood smoke filled the air, and a man walked through the neighborhood at night clicking two wooden blocks to remind people to put out fires and turn off space heaters.

Sensei's heaters pulsed like beacons at our feet as I began learning shamisen in earnest after the concert in Kamakura. I took the trains to her house on weekends, walking the big road alone, where the ginkgo's leaves shimmered like tiny fans, and paulownia leaves fell big as baseball mitts, red maples tiny as a fingernail.

Sometimes when I arrived we would pick up Sensei's order from a local co-op and I would carry the Styrofoam container back to her apartment where she'd put everything away. Going to the grocery store was a waste of time. Cleanliness was a priority. She washed her hands before touching the instruments and asked that I do, too. She hopped down from her stool after meals to wipe the floor with a rag and then paced in the kitchen brushing her teeth afterward.

After any performance was what Sensei called *soraori*, "sky falling," the inevitable return to daily life. While I was going about my teaching and taking Larry to the noh play in Odawara, trying to linger in my moment on stage as long as possible, Sensei had boarded a bullet train to Kyoto and brought back an ancient drum. She pointed out its two honeyed skins lashed with orange hemp ropes. The body of the drum, which was shaped like a free weight, was painted with black lacquer and gold paint.

"I need adventure," she had said.

I wondered if travel helped her leave behind the concert, or savor it more. When I arrived for a lesson the next week, she looked refreshed in navy slacks and a green tee shirt with a red Mao star. I brought her *kamaboko*, a loaf of fish paste from Odawara, which she gratefully swapped in the fridge for a pitcher of cold barley tea.

On the music table was my new shamisen. Next to it and laid out like a dentist's tools were a navy knit finger sling and matching sticky pad for my lap, a plastic bridge to insert under the strings, one heavy oak pick, and a red velvet dusting cloth. In a black zippered pouch was a pitch wheel with a piece of surgical tape and my name on it written in Sensei's disconnected cursive script.

"Meet your shamisen," she said.

Sensei had several shamisen hanging on the walls. Any one of them might be prepared and readied for my lessons. They all looked similar, but there were ones I steered clear of, that she'd lay down for me to play and I'd cringe. If I requested another she would say, "What's wrong?" If I made excuses, "This shamisen is hard to play" or "This one has a short neck," she would look dubious. "Shamisen is shamisen, Janet." To her, it was always up to you, the player. The instrument picked up your playing habits and style—"your personality," she said—like the nib of a fountain pen.

My shamisen was an affordable practice model made of *karin*, red oak, a pale auburn with a grainy swirl along the neck. It cost about $400. Sensei's were made of *kouki*, red sandalwood, and cost ten times that. My tuning pegs were black sandalwood, hers were ivory. My sound box was covered with dog skin (cheaper and more durable), hers cat. The throaty buzz of the first string was identical. It made the whole instrument vibrate.

"I love it," I said, and I did.

Without delay, she started me on my first piece, *Suehirogari*, "The Fool and the Folding Fan," a non-beginner piece since there were no beginner pieces for the shamisen. No scales or warm-ups, either. Only whole songs to jump into, imitating the master.

A model was especially helpful when trying to find finger positions, which were found not by fret but intuition. They were called *kandokoro*, "intuitive places." You found them by sensing proportions and distance, rather than some technique or formula.

It took a year to master them, common wisdom said.

Tuning took three. For now, Sensei hopped off her stool to crank one of my pegs higher or lower when our strings started to clash. She cared less about our being perfectly in tune than perfectly in synch. *Ma* continued to be the thing she cared about. Every song had new *ma.* It could only be taught by the bruising method of pruning a player's playing in real time.

Why was the shamisen allowed to remain so unruly? I wondered. Why hadn't someone devised frets? Secured the tuning pegs? Added lines for positions? I was always searching for excuses. Some teachers taught by pasting a clear plastic label of positions along the neck. "You will never be independent," Sensei said. "Harder to learn this way, but please try."

I came to her house as often as I could. I could see no reason not to, nor could she. Learning meant side-by-side playing, for hours, between small talk and breaks to pick up her co-op goods. I would arrive and she would instruct me, and at the dinner hour she made a "poor meal"—rice and pickles, a piece of fish and some vacuum-packed Western thing that was truly atrocious: a foil bag of crinkle-cut French fries, chicken wings; perhaps she thought it would comfort us or she was curious about their tastes—talking while she navigated with her long chopsticks, asking about my day, guiding our talks with *We never know future,* and *We can do many things.*

I was soothed by Sensei's kitchen movements as much as her music. Trout sushi from her hometown on the Sea of Japan, creamy pumpkin salad, crunchy cucumbers dressed with bonito flakes. The way she reached for the tea kettle, holding her kimono sleeve away, and handled the long bamboo chopsticks, plucking each piece of sushi from the box. The way she sprinkled leaves for tea and fanned slices of fruit. Nothing was rushed, loud, or excessive. There was control and care in everything she did. That was what I wanted. *That.*

I wanted to care about something that much. To know what mattered, what to hope. I wanted to know what I wanted in life.

After the concert, it was like I couldn't get back into a box again, something had sprung, and I sought connection now in all the unknown places of Japan, where I might find more of what I wanted. Larry now equaled "going back," to the States, to my mother's house, where I would always be too loud, too screechy, too everything I'd heard growing up.

Inside music I was happiest. The outside world bore no relation to it, and was untenable. Sensei could have been speaking for me when she said, "I don't want ordinary life." But she'd found a way to navigate both, to have a life full of music and people, art, and plans— oh I wanted that! At the time the best way forward seemed to be to stay, to take on her mantle and mission. To follow her example. In life as on the shamisen.

≡

The breakup with Larry happened quickly, after a kabuki show with Sensei that Larry had mostly slept through. The play, *Shunkan*, was about a man who sacrifices himself to exile so the lovers can be together.

How could I explain to him, much less myself, that this was what I'd been looking for? This tiny Japanese woman with a Cleopatra bob who served the most delicious rice I'd ever tasted, who had shamisen, rows of them, whose sound was my very heart? That I could be buzzed with its sadness, delighted by its weight. That this music and teacher understood me in a way he never would?

Music was about my spirit, she'd said.

Most awkwardly, how to explain that whenever he touched me now I felt a hint of betrayal? I thought of Sensei in her rooms, taking down one of her long slender shamisen and gently coaxing it into sound.

When we got home from the performance, I sat on the edge of the bed and Larry stood in the kitchen, and through the open sliding door I told him that I didn't want to return to the States. He offered to stay in Japan. No, I said gently. I didn't want that, either.

Since early November, Sensei and I had been visiting realtors in Tokyo, looking for an *oyasan*, landlord, open-minded enough to rent to a gaijin, "outside person." She wanted me closer to her, in an apartment nearby instead of two hours away, like an *uchideshi*, a live-in disciple, allowing for unfettered fusion of art and life.

Sensei was embarrassed that many landlords hung up when they heard the room was for a foreigner.

"Can you believe?" she would say, squinting and shaking her head, and then sigh. "But this is Japan."

Sensei tried to convince realtors that I was safe and trustworthy by bringing out a slim photo album from her tote bag and flipping to a picture of me backstage in the black kimono.

I loved Japanese shamisen. I'd already performed, she told the realtor. I had another concert lined up for next March. I wasn't going anywhere.

"Ehhh …", the realtors said as Sensei flipped the pages of her gaijin students, their faces registering something new, like a coin in a pay phone bringing up the dial tone.

Convenience was of utmost importance to Sensei, which meant being close to downtown Tokyo to work and close to her to play music. *You can save a time. You should save your energy.* Her prescriptions for me were like welcome foods, nourishing and true.

After a few tries, we found a six-mat Japanese room in a flimsy wooden building with an ugly metal door. Inside was a square of space to unlace your shoes and step up to a four-mat kitchen (to say my apartment was laid out in mats made my heart leap). A washer was squeezed in the corner of the kitchen. I would hang clothes to dry them. There was a dorm-sized fridge and a two-burner camp stove. With no hot water, I would boil water and keep it in a thermos to do dishes, and heat the bath with a gas heater as the Japanese did, rinsing outside the tub before entering the scalding water.

Sensei didn't approve. Tatami was dirty. Mites would nest in the straw matting in cold weather or the rainy season. Wood was not as safe as concrete. A shower would save my time. Worst was the toilet in the same room as the tub, though one step up. "Your throne," she said, fascinated.

The landlord was difficult. I would pay rent to him and his wife in person, offering a purple receipt book for their stamp, on the same day every month. The rent was six hundred dollars, sixty-three thousand yen, laughably cheap for Tokyo.

The landlord arrived to show the apartment in a kimono, a thin obi sitting low on his hips. He crossed his arms and politely grilled

Sensei as we looked around the rooms. Could I keep a contract? Was I noisy? Did I have boyfriends? Sensei stiffened, releasing her words in terse syllables. I heard her mention shamisen, and he looked at me. Sensei had her hand on the photo album in her tote, as if she was debating taking it out, and just as she was lifting it I saw for the first time some words along the spine. She pushed it deeper into her bag before I understood what she had written in her distinctive cursive script: My Universe.

As we walked to her house for a lesson afterward, she boiled darkly. He had humiliated her, questioned her very existence.

"Let's not take it then. I don't want you to have to deal with him. Something else will turn up."

She shook her head. By the next week, she was convinced. Nothing was perfect. We should take it.

It was now December, the end of the semester drawing near. Larry tried to change my mind about breaking up.

"I'll be more social. Maybe I'll take up shamisen, too."

"You won't even sing out loud." I shook my head. "You can't change for me."

I went to my sock drawer and started rummaging. I'd be in sock feet in important places now. Holes wouldn't do. My fingers ran across my singing fan. Sensei had let me keep it. The lacquer rib was smooth and cool under my thumb.

"I'm going to stay here and study music," I said, and threw a pair of argyles into the trash.

I think one of us cried, or both of us, and then we promised to be friends forever. That night, lying in the dark, back to back, he said, "Miss Janet?" using an old nickname for me. "Do me a favor?"

"Sure," I said.

"Become the best goddam foreign shamisen player that ever was."

He was being sentimental and generous, and it was part of his character to be this way. But I heard in his words a caveat: that to give up a future life together—a normal life, marriage, kids—it had better be worth it.

On the last evening of our teaching program there was a party in Roppongi in Tokyo with meals on trays and lots of booze. The president groped us in pictures. Teachers were talking about their next gig, and griping about students. "Can you believe I asked them to draw a cat and they all drew it in exactly the same way, stroke for stroke? Creepy."

It was the gaijin ghetto, I decided. I wanted nothing to do with lost hopeless people. I was tethered now. The leaving of the party was an echo of leaving Larry. The night was bleak and cold and felt like the end of something.

That night, I copied out a long quote from *Flow* by Mihaly Csikszentmihalyi. "The notion of family life typically implies constraint, responsibilities that interfere with one's goals and freedom of action…. Rules and obligations … exclude … a wide range of possibilities so that we might concentrate fully on a selected set of options."

He was talking about marriage as a way in which this kind of commitment, obligation, or duty could be realized.

"By making up one's mind to invest psychic energy exclusively … regardless of any problems, obstacles, or more attractive options that may come along later, one is freed of the constant pressure of trying to maximize emotional returns…. As a result, a great deal of energy gets freed up for living, instead of being spent on wondering about how to live."

I circled on the page next a quote that shocked me, and which would have new resonance in Japan. *Accepting limitations is liberating.*

=

Sensei pressed her identity seal in the dotted circle and lifted. I followed, scrunching as much of my Western signature as possible into page after page of the little circles. Sensei was my guarantor, which meant she would be responsible financially if I bolted. She was also loaning me the "key money"—an extra fee she called a "bribe"— of several thousand dollars. I barely had first and last month's rent.

"Don't worry, you can pay anytime," she said. "Money is not important. Do what you want first. Money follows you."

After signing the contract, we bundled against the chill, thanked the realtor, a kind man, and walked out into the wintry night of Shimokitazawa. Chinese noodles in pork broth were simmering nearby. Along the tiny twisted streets back to the station, boys in baggy pants skateboarded by. Brown-haired girls were giggling in arcades and gathering tiny photos coming out of a machine. An occasional child wandered by with no parent, shoulders sagging under his enormous backpack, his small steps leading him through the teenaged crowds.

We took the train one stop to her neighborhood in Daita. It was quiet. The tofu vats silent in the little shop across the street. The international grocer's shutter down and no steaming samples of coffee in the air.

Instead of walking down the big road we crossed over to the other side on a pedestrian bridge that exited into a shrine. The dirt-packed grounds were shadowy, the stages shuttered.

"Hmmm ... " she said, looking around. "Maybe nice performance here someday."

Her coat had extra-large buttons, dwarfing her tiny figure. The only giveaway to her secret life was an earphone dangling from her music tote. As we walked, she was oblivious to it. At the karaoke bar, we stopped and peered down the road at the bank of apartments.

"Your nest," she said now, as if something was just dawning on her.

She turned around and pointed across the road, to wooden placards peeking out behind the concrete wall of a graveyard. "There is Yamada-sensei's grave." Her teacher's teacher.

"This is Shamisen Ward," she said, looking up at me. "Like a destiny," she said.

The word beckoned like a doorbell chime.

I nodded and squinted into the twilight.

PART II

6

… the context in which it bloomed and fired …

Sensei had a small discolored patch on her right forearm from where it had rested on the shamisen's sound box for thirty years.

"My Sensei has, too," she said, rubbing it.

I would sometimes check my own arm when pushing up the knitted sleeve of a sweater, preparing to play, and think I saw some small shadow forming there. How long did it take for one's body to be permanently marked by sound? It was like the shamisen became part of you, grown out from lap and limbs.

This made sense to me. The shamisen was animate in a way other instruments I had played were not. My immovable piano, the cold brass of a trombone in high school, one year of the hard silver flute. But the shamisen: pick it up and it responded. The goal was to stay still while it slipped and slid, to temper and tame it, and myself along with it.

But who can stand an instrument that veers and dives, evilly, on your knees, like a naughty child, a wayward imp?

There were two choices here. One could give up—how often I have wanted to throw the shamisen, Sensei, everything I have inside me of Japan, out the window! The adjustments are endless, the back and forth wearying, and costly.

The other option is to plod onward, one tiny adjustment at a time. One could learn to listen. To bear the slow dripping away of feeling from your legs when on the knees. One could stand not knowing where any of it was going. One could learn to live with impossibility.

≡

Tokyo's winter is indoors. Although temperatures rarely dip below freezing and the appearance of snow or ice is rare, houses have no central heating. The only warmth is local: heated train seats, pocket hand warmers, steaming noodles, scalding baths. One kept moving, thawing at each new source of friendly heat.

When I returned to Tokyo after a quick Christmas visit home, the city was quiet. Most Japanese were celebrating the New Year's holiday with family, drinking sake and reading *nengajo*, ritual greeting cards hand-delivered on New Year's Day. Sensei's house was devoid of decoration. She spent the holiday at her teacher's house cooking and cleaning. For herself she prepared only *zoni*, a clear broth with bites of fancy sticky rice.

Family and friends worried about my wandering. Why was I staying in Japan? "Can you trust this woman?" my mother asked. "It's music, Mom," I said. "She's a teacher." They were seeing me as perhaps as I had seen my friend Amy, who signed her postcards from Japan in a foreign script. It was distressing to see her name suddenly dissembled into a series of vertical and horizontal lines I couldn't decode. Part of her was gone, her life now apart from me. I wonder if my own family began to see me this way then, or perhaps always had, a life off-kilter, something always held back, a private *ma*.

It was cold as I changed trains from the airport at Tokyo Station. I hurried along with my bags onto the heated train seats, stopping for a hot can of tea in a vending machine. I boarded local trains and took my time, happy with my local heat sources, savoring the destination: Setagaya-Daita 3-1-150. Setagaya was the ward, Daita the area, 3 the district, 1 the central building from which all others fanned out. More like lottery numbers than addresses, this was how Tokyo organized its nameless circular streets: an endless burrowing into the core.

In my absence, my rooms had been visited by Sensei and Yamaguchi-san, a rich housewife who admired her work and wanted to help. I arrived to find cotton futons patterned with colorful fans, gold-threaded floor cushions, Dior blankets, an electric carpet, an electric thermos, a terrycloth toilet seat cover, and a *kotatsu*, a small table with a heater underneath. The top could be removed to sandwich a quilt in between, turning it into a little Mount Fuji to warm your legs. "Nice stuff," Sensei said, happier about the time she had saved me shopping than the designer goods. It meant more time to train me. Our next performance was in March.

My shamisen was there, in a handsome shamisen stand that Sensei had found at an antique fair, a cypress box where two could stand upright. "There might be some treasure," she said when I called to thank her. The phone line was hers, too. She had an extra from one of her daughters. One had to buy the line in Japan, from the national company, which had a monopoly.

"Is there some drawer?" she asked. There was, a slender one at the bottom of the stand. Inside was a very old *koma* box that contained, in slots, three very fine bridges, a wooden one for practice and two ivory of varying heights, with initials written on the back in black ink. There was also a newer box containing a tiny sliver of wood on a cord. I could hear Sensei nodding through the phone. "Capo," she said. "The person must have been a good player. Someday I can show you how to use."

She also left me an ashtray (though she encouraged me to quit), a package of my favorite caffeinated peppermints, a tea kettle, a coffee filter and mug, clips for hanging futons and laundry, and a wall calendar to organize my time.

Part of the phone was a fax machine, which everyone used back then to send maps to get around Tokyo. We had no Google or GPS. No one carried smart phones or laptops. I didn't surf the internet to look for shamisen websites or scan YouTube for sound files. During my nearly four years with Sensei, I recorded everything on flimsy cassette reels that could snag or tear in the machine. Later I used mini discs, and finally a digital recorder.

Back then there was only Sensei and me. My immersion was total. It was the only way.

And so the fact that everything in my rooms was hers was

natural. There was little that I would acquire over the next few years that was not.

≡

Sensei used an oversized Tokyo Gas Company calendar on the kitchen wall for her lesson schedule. As you were leaving, she stood in front of it, and, with the pen dangling on the string next to it, wrote in your next lesson time. By late January, a new batch of foreign names filled the boxes and, in the white space all around, English words to feed her hunger for metaphor: "Achilles heel," "sounding board," "Miles to go before I sleep."

Students came from all over Tokyo and its suburbs, and from as far away as Sendai or Nagoya, to take her up on her offer of free instruction. Her students were actors, art dealers, newscasters, teachers, tourists, didgeridoo players, bankers, missionaries, and, for a time the great-granddaughter of Lilian Gish. Each one was "amazing," she said at the kitchen table, where she liked to dig into their characters. "Shami-psychology," she joked but was serious. Could they correct their mistakes? Or did they repeat them over and over? Did they get *ma*? Or did they have to be told to wait, again and again?

There was music in Sensei's rooms nearly every weeknight. She traveled by bus home from work, where on her lunch hour she may have made notation for a new student, or answered a new inquiry about her ad. These sometimes came in by fax as we practiced, the loud beep kicking in after one ring, and then the scratchy hum of the paper curling out of the machine and, with another beep, falling to the floor like a chocolate shaving.

When Sensei arrived home from work she would eat a rice ball at the sink, washing it down with a cup of green tea, and then remove her apron, brush her teeth, wash her hands, and prepare the instruments. During a lesson would often come a longer time to talk and eat. Eating was for survival, not pleasure (unless you were eating the *kurotani* lunchbox atop the Ginza Core building, her favorite lunch). Her energy lasted until around nine o'clock, when she would stretch her wrist and look at the calendar and ask, "Is next Monday good time for you?" signaling that the student should pack their score and heavy pick, the finger sling, and the lap pad in the wrapping cloth she had given them. Sensei was excellent at conversation until the last, when the student was lacing up their shoes in the *genkan*. She always had a plan for music, an outing, some arrangement to be made, like the patterns in our scores.

On weekends the music hardly stopped. She filled the hours with one student after another, each walking down the long concrete veranda to her door, past the old people who lived all around her. A man next door with dementia sometimes wandered up and down the corridor. Sensei pulled you in the door. "Is he there?" she would ask. "So uncomfortable."

She did not like the old. When I once mimicked the humped backs of old farm women in the city—for she loved to laugh when I did silly things, like peel my socks off my heels when I was hot—she looked terrified and told me to stop.

One student lesson bled into the next. There were more and more to train, the March concert to prepare them for. Without this constant stream of people, making her rooms something of a YMCA on the weekends, I think she would have slowly unwound like a clock and stopped moving. She "seduced" students, she said. Her lure was access, experience, and redemption from the Japanese fantasy that gaijin sat around at cafes all day sipping lattes. "You have a reason to be here," she said. Music was honorable. We were doing something important.

I didn't think her "seduction" applied to me, but it did. My schedule revolved around our lessons, and I shuttled often down the big road in the wintry air, music bundle hugged to my chest, to where she was waiting in her rooms, her hair a smooth curtain, her inky eyes warm with humor, and the space heaters pulsing at our feet. It was no different from any number of times when I'd been taken with a new romance.

In fact, it all had a slightly erotic charge to it. She talked about a student "dumping" her, about having a "crush" on a piece of music.

Once, when a student overslept and missed a lesson, she said, "He slept over," and when told the real meaning, laughed and repeated the joke often. She didn't seem interested in romance in real life. But the hint of it was fun, playful, and perhaps more important than the real thing.

Sometimes when I showed up for a lesson, I would be deflated to find Sensei sitting with the previous student, listening with her sharp dark eyes on the person, sorting out a problem, like an expiring visa or a cheating girlfriend. ("Women are demons," she kept reminding me.) I heard her repeating what she'd told me about the unfairness of Japanese life, the fifteen-minute shamisen lesson. Who can learn?

She seduced everyone the same way. *So gorgeous. More important to join. We should enjoy.* And maybe she slid a snow-white tabi onto their feet, overlaid their natural shape with a new one: artful, pure, snug.

Sometimes Sensei would call me and ask, "Can you come Saturday for group lesson? You inspire them to learn harder." My own lessons were whizzing along—I went as often as I could; this was the benefit of the nearby *uchideshi*—but she needed to train many. I became their "rival." Rivals, my students told me, were necessary for them to advance in their studies, and in life. Rather than an obstacle, a rival showed them the way. The Japanese didn't demolish their competition, they used it.

I had completed *Suehirogari*, including the devilish *chirashi* movement. Literally meaning "scattering," the *chirashi* appeared near the end. Here, the orchestra careened into a kind of controlled chaos, each instrument following its own course—singer, shamisen, drummers, flute—not in harmony, not in dissonance, not rising to a climax, not staying the same. It was as if all the strands of music needed to express themselves urgently, and did so, tangling and untangling until suddenly all sound peeled away and a sole shamisen note signaled the end.

To keep me busy, Sensei taught me small geisha songs, folk ballads, and a flashy duet from *Musume Dojoji*, the dance of the jealous woman turning into a snake ghost. I played these songs with her when new students came. If they saw me doing it, she said, they would want to, too. In this way, I colluded in her seductions.

But at group lessons, which happened on the weekends, when Sensei's floors were covered with cushions, finger slings, scores, and tea trays full of empty sweets wrappers—"So messy," she would say, breathless. "Just all toys!"—I often found myself staring off into the colorful stacks of music on her shelf, or eyeing the hard square lines of written kanji among the loopy script of foreign names on the gas calendar, learning the characters for shamisen, literally "three, taste, string," when it appeared to mark her twice-monthly lesson. Or I excused myself and went to the toilet, lingering there to stare at the map of Edo, old Tokyo, curling at the edges.

And then I would be struck with shame. How could Sensei not want lots of students? Attrition was vicious. I was surprised by the number of them that arrived. By their care, by their jokes, by their interest. I was sure they would depart soon, and it was often true, sometimes with one of Sensei's loaned shamisen on the back of their bicycle scooter. "Waste of time," was all she said.

As the music grew livelier, Sensei emerged into her own power, less the solitary monk of my first impressions and more a woman of calculated effect. It was due to the men, I think. She doted on the male students who hovered awkwardly over the shamisen, their large hands gripping the pick like footballs, fingers getting tangled in the strings. They looked less like they were playing the shamisen than throttling it. They required L-sized knit finger slings and extra-large kimono, which were hard to find and were never long enough. They high-fived. "Level up!"

The men teased out of her a love for Pat Boone, her hiking expeditions into the mountains as a girl to take photographs. Where the girls brought her votive candles and pretty paper, the men brought her jazz CDs and bottles of Johnny Walker Red.

One night came a student she had never seen the likes of. He had the brains of a professor, but looked like a surfer. He played rock-a-billy riffs on the shamisen but studied imperial court music. His teacher played at Meiji Shrine, and lived a stone's throw from Sensei's house. One cold night in January, she called me to her house to come meet him.

≡

It might seem from what I've written that I was obsessed with Sensei and not taken with other things. This was not wholly true. I liked Tokyo and spent days wandering through its streets, much as I had in Odawara, swooning at the simplest things: coming upon a master sandal maker in his shop and watching him carve and sand a perfect wooden sole. A housewife on her bicycle at dusk, her dark hair coiled on her head, her white blouse crisply ironed.

Attuned as I was to the shamisen—its tilting rhythms and silent spaces—it influenced everything I experienced. The *ma* in conversations. The love of puns and imagery. I hedged, said maybe, started holding onto my questions. It's not that I chose to pursue only Japanese ways, but since first hearing the shamisen, they adhered. Packed onto the trains in the mornings to go to the English school where I now worked in Shinjuku, I wondered if anyone could hear Sensei's music through my headphones—the halting pained bleating, the tense buzzing sadness—sounds that I tapped like a mainline into some collective experience.

I stopped reading, which even now shocks me. I had never gone anywhere without a book. It was my natural home, the place I loved best, along with the piano. But in Tokyo, reading took me out of experience. Reading felt now the way it had always felt to my mother, perhaps, when she called to me to get my nose out of a book, there was a table to set.

Sound was king. The ear how I took in everything. Not only music but all of Tokyo. The train chimes, a million pairs of shoes on the station steps, vendors hawking their wares. Tokyo was a carnival, a free-for-all bazaar. Glass and concrete towers dwarfed kimono makers. Video towers stood next to three-hundred-year-old incense shops. The contrast was itchy, like the shamisen's restless tuning.

I was moved by everything. The kazoo of the tofu seller as he passed Sensei's house in the afternoon, and the jingle of house keys in the aprons of housewives who went out to buy loaves from the wooden box lashed to his bicycle. The song of the sweet potato vendor and the laundry pole seller pricked me on some primitive level, where the shamisen was like a strong perfume, the scent of blood I was on the trail of, heartbeat quickening.

It's hard to describe how I absorbed everything. Nuance, texture, mood, indecision. Attunement wasn't something I could turn off after a lesson. Learning required an openness at all times—a lesson could appear anywhere, on the train, over sushi. Like the proverbial tree falling in the forest, you had to be there to catch it.

And if I felt lonely at times, for conversations of the deep, exploring variety, or for human contact, as I did sometimes on the crowded trains—so near the suits, the oiled hair, the liquid eyes, wanting one to slip an arm around my waist in a gesture of familiarity—it soon turned to "loneliness," a state of being that everyone shared. Sadness was prized in Japan, *sabishisa* to be courted. Perhaps it is romantic to elevate loneliness to this degree, to say that sadness was welcome, and this is not quite what I am saying. What was new was the possibility that these things were not to be avoided or cured. Melancholy was useful.

All I had to do was go back to my six-mat room, slide open the *fusuma*, and pad silently across the mats to my shamisen. Slide it out from where it stood in its ancient wooden holder, the sound of the silk bag rustling as its paleness came into view, the soft click as the three strings popped into their slots on the bridge.

I did not devise my own way to prepare the instrument. Did not vary the procedure an inch from what Sensei had instructed me that first day. It never occurred to me to try. Part of playing the shamisen was about this very fact. I need do nothing else. There was no new thing to add. A procedure had been laid in place for hundreds of years. Playing the shamisen was like stepping into a stream with its own currents and ancient pathways, and all you had to do was be absorbed into its gentle curling flow.

Music before had been something I had tried to master. Entering a tradition—inexorable and true—felt like letting something master me.

≡

About Kenneth, Sensei had said on the phone, "Very important person." He was an ethnomusicologist and knew something about Asian music. When I arrived at her rooms to meet him, Sensei was chatting with a handyman replacing a lightbulb in her kitchen.

"Izumi-san," she said, introducing us. He knew all about me: another foreigner who played shamisen.

Sensei swung the skirt of her jumper. "I need a man for some things."

"Oh, geez, no you don't. You're just too short," I said.

She flashed her eyes at me.

"*Erai,*" Izumi-san said of my shamisen studies, "good girl."

A knock rattled the steel door.

"*Dozo!*" Sensei called out.

A man in black jeans and a short-sleeved shirt entered the *genkan* under a heavy backpack, which he loosened and dropped to the floor, shaking a salt-and-pepper lock of hair out of his eyes and bowing.

"*Konban wa,*" he said.

Sensei turned to me, her mouth in an "O."

"Please, too formal," she said, waving him into the room. "Would you like some tea?"

We settled into the music room while Izumi-san finished up. Sensei lowered the music table so we could sit around it, Japanese-style, on our knees, and talk. Sensei looked like a tiny duchess from the past holding court while Kenneth told us his background. She entered deep-listening mode, moving little, eyes looking not down into her folded hands but straight ahead in ever-widening pools, hitching "mmmms" and "ehhhhs" to the ends of his phrases. Who was his teacher? What genres of music had he studied?

Though versed in Balinese gamelan music, Kenneth's musical studies centered around *gagaku,* tenth-century Japanese imperial court music. Her coal eyes blazed. "All connected."

"Are you a musician?" he asked, noticing me, it seemed, for the first time.

"She has already performed," Sensei said. "As a singer."

I shifted on my knees.

Sensei seemed fascinated by all aspects of Kenneth, the puns he made on train stops (Ikebukuro, "bag lake"; Roppongi, "six hills"; Yotsuya, "cat skin seller"—Sensei shook her head at this last one, "Different kanji"), the rooming house where he lived. Maybe he wanted to get a place in the neighborhood?

He was a good musician—he sailed through the first pages of "The Fool and his Fan" with ease; Sensei recruited him for the March concert—but I was irritated, irritated at how at home he made himself in her rooms, irritated at how he strummed the shamisen too hard, cracking violently at the skin, with no tender ear for *ma.*

At one point, he demonstrated his *hichiriki,* a tiny end-blown flute, asking Sensei for a cup of hot green tea to soften the reed. Even Sensei had rarely heard imperial court music. Kenneth sat in the empty middle room cross-legged (men could get away with this in Japan, women never), dipped the reed in the tea, and then, passing air through the small tube, clouded the room with a high-pitched wheeze like a kazoo. Sensei was motionless, her eyes cast down, as if waiting for the emperor to pass.

I kept checking in to see if she had noticed anything unusual, for some conspiratorial glance between us. I knew Japanese women often had no critical faculty to assess Western men. American men who could not get dates at home were sought after in Japan, seen as liberated, uncomplicated, physical. Even a nerdy man I had taught with who had danced powwows on a cruise ship had a girlfriend. Another who wore a leather jacket embossed with Bugs Bunny was soon dating a high school girl after arriving. This phenomenon was so common there was a popular comic strip about it called

"Charisma Man!" His enemy was his cover-blowing anathema, Western Woman.

But no glance came.

Before Kenneth left, Sensei inked in another lesson on the gas calendar and handed him a persimmon for his journey. He flashed a smile and got busily harnessed under his backpack and laced up his black sneakers.

After he left, we sat at the little table in the kitchen, waiting for the kettle to boil. Sensei pushed the lacquer bowl of snacks toward me.

"He knows this music. Amazing. We can do many things."

Her voice got low and dreamy. She talked of forming her own group, of a total break with Japanese musical society.

"Our own concert. We don't need dragon ladies."

She was in the snow globe again, distant, but this time not aboil, just scheming.

"What do you think?"

"Very talented," I said, and saw an ocean, waves, a giant whale with only one small part breaching the surface.

7

... a complete unstringing of the day ...

Sensei could be bitter out of nowhere. This, too, was part of her essential nature. She looked at the Japanese world around her and at its daily life as antagonistic to her dreams, oppressive and narrow-minded.

Seeing herself as distant and opposed explained why when I saw her on the street when we were out in Tokyo, she looked different from everyone around her. In her pinwheel velour Beatles cap and oiled bob framing her face, her tiny hands and feet, she appeared like an exotic bird returned from a long migration elsewhere. Child-woman, neither fully formed. A sprite with her elfin nature, her barbs and jokes, but always dignity.

One Saturday afternoon, during a group rehearsal, the phone rang. It took a while to locate it, and finally, Sensei unearthed it from a pile of scores on the floor.

"*Moshi moshi*," she said, her voice soft and fragile.

It was February 1997. The plums had blossomed and the ritual ousting of demons and wishing of good luck into all corners of the house known as Setsubun passed. Doug, Kenneth, and I were joined by Jane, a Canadian cellist; Lena, an off-and-on student who refused to wear a kimono; Brian, a half-Japanese searching for his birth mother; and, at the last minute, Alan, a theater director from Milwaukee. Many of us lived in the neighborhood. It really was becoming the "Shamisen Ward" Sensei joked about. She installed Kenneth in a six-mat room over a futon seller a few blocks away.

Sensei walked into the kitchen to take the call and everyone rolled off their knees to stretch. I could see that it was a Japanese caller because her head was bobbing in symbolic bows. She said, *"Hai, wakarimashita"* "Yes, yes, of course," and used long polite forms, not the clipped sleepy syllables she used when her daughters called to say good night during evening lessons. She listened more than spoke. Finally, she put the phone down and came back.

"That was the Queen."

Who was the Queen?

Lena piped up. "In last year's concert the Queen gave Sensei no credit. We played better than her students!"

Who was this lady? we wanted to know. Suddenly there were stakes.

The Queen was the shamisen teacher of the students at International University, who we'd be performing with in two weeks. She was also the wife of an ambassador.

"Housewife," Sensei added.

These encounters always darkened her mood. The Queen wanted to be sure Sensei's students were ready. She asked about whether they would need her for tuning the instruments or any supplies. She was basically erasing Sensei as our teacher.

"I am human being," Sensei said. "I didn't say anything. I am just teaching shamisen."

She claimed this happened often, this kind of censure, of insult. We didn't want to perform with the Queen. Why did we need her?

But we did, Sensei said. We needed performance opportunities. Otherwise, our music had no meaning.

Often it was this way: no solution, only an indignity to endure.

=

The difficulty of shamisen music often had to do with time. Each piece had its own *ma*, spaces, and its own quality of *merihari*. *Merihari*, Sensei explained, was the gently uneven, natural-sounding but highly constructed quick-slow tempo of her music. She explained it, "Slow, like when someone dies, then quick, like going to a lover."

There was no way to absorb this other than by imitating it with tapes or in her rooms. I always felt she knew when I hadn't practiced: when my strumming was abrupt, my "intuitive places" inaccurate, and when my handle on a piece's *ma* shaky, my hands and heart not yet scored by the spaces.

I knew I wasn't Sensei's only student. But I expected to feel like I was. I thought at lessons she would be absorbed in my playing, meticulously scouring it, tending to it, finding ways I could improve it. But after playing, we ended up at the little table in the kitchen, talking about a student or a new plan for an outing or concert.

During group lessons, I was again struck by her hands or her hair. Her strands looked the same every time I saw her, except every four weeks or so when the line at her neck was a little higher and more severe. The hands were tiny and nearly cupped, as if holding a shamisen at all times. They were always clean, the nails neatly trimmed, dry, ready. Hands of use and purpose.

This was a way to hold on to her, I suppose. To make her private again. I feared losing her. I depended on her for so much already.

When she suggested I practice with Lena one day, I objected.

"Why? She lives not far from you. Maybe fun, playing music together."

I was skeptical. Lena was hotheaded and temperamental. She looked awkward with a shamisen. What could I learn from her, a foreigner? But I agreed, trying to be a "team player."

Lena lived in the opposite direction from Sensei, and the following Saturday I walked up to her house to practice. I carried my shamisen, something I never did, playing one of several of Sensei's superior instruments at lessons or concerts. It felt strange to remove it from my rooms and carry it down the busy street. I hugged it along my flank in the long red nylon bag that looked like it contained a set of oars or golf clubs. Bicycles whizzed past and trucks and buses cruised down the busy four-lane road. The convenience stores were unfamiliar, the sidewalk wider. I had to use an overhead walkway to get across an intersection.

We set up our shamisen in her room. Lena sat on her bed and I sat at her desk, where I smoothed open my score on top of the books, papers, notes, and maps.

"OK, can we just go back and do that again?" Lena asked after we made it through the opening passage.

"Sure," I said.

Without a singer, the shamisen sounded bare, denuded of the full power of its emotion. It was harder to keep time, too. There was no second parallel line to interact with. No way to gauge tempo.

When we reached the end—out of synch and out of tune— Lena jumped up to make us some tea.

I stretched my wrist and looked around at her desk. There were immigration papers, guidebooks.

"She likes women," Sensei had teased me on the phone that morning before I headed out. It was as if she couldn't address the shamisen without a frisson of the erotic.

Lena appeared with two mugs, not Japanese teacups on a tray. We sipped British tea and talked a little. Lena's family was from Russia and she spoke Russian. Lena teased Sensei with Russian quips sometimes, and jokingly called her a communist spy.

"Why did you come back to Japan?" I asked.

She sipped her tea. She'd come back for a woman. To be with women, it seemed, though she didn't say. I didn't know if the woman was Japanese or foreign and didn't ask. But I could see coming back for a person. For love.

She continued to say there was something that she hadn't finished here and wanted to come back to see what it was.

"What do you think that is?"

"I dunno," she said. "It's just a feeling I have. Life in the States doesn't hold anything for me now."

Leaving Japan, a friend had said, was "like quitting a drug. If you can stay away a year, you're in the clear."

I was no longer thinking of leaving. I wanted only to get more woven into Japanese life, whose thousand gestures filled me with yearning, like the bows of luggage handlers and gas attendants, their shiny exposed crowns filling me with gratitude. Service, duty, humility. I was in awe of the human spirit, its firmness and solidity. They gave me a kind of hope. Through the endless shaping of the human spirit and the riddle of ritual, I felt human and alive. Through elaborate artifice, one could find oneself.

=

At this time, I began to know something of Japan's history. Edo, the over-two-hundred-year period of isolation; Meiji, the West entering Japan; Taisho, a brief peaceful mingling of East and West; and then Showa and the era of war. Mostly it was Edo I knew, the eighteenth and nineteenth centuries, when Tokyo was the capital of Japan, and when our music was composed.

Sensei's rooms were steeped in Edo. Faces of geisha and maiko adorned hand towels. Painted faces of samurai stared out from a kabuki calendar in the kitchen. No clock was correct but for the blue winking lights of the VCR at our feet. If you asked what time it was, Sensei would laugh and say, "You are on Edo time."

In the middle of a lesson, she might take down the Edo Encyclopedia and start scanning, her pick in hand, flicking the air. "Hmmm …," she would say, smoothing out the pages. She was a school girl again, her webbed finger sling on her left hand, gliding along the page. "Tenpo II, very restricted period." In that moment I was transported to a new place with her, one I never imagined existing.

Ruled by strict shoguns who banned luxury, an aesthetic of hiddenness arose in Edo. People made puns instead of speaking directly. They lined the inside of bland kimono with colorful paintings. *Iki*, sophisticated restraint, was the ethos of the day. *Iki* was a desirable yearning that didn't need to be consummated. That would be *yabo*, boorish, not because it was sexual but because it was literal. *Iki* was not romance, it was Eros.

Romance has a dreamy quality, and is what I often felt in Tokyo. Taking a bullet train to a hot spring and ordering a bento from the stewardess as she came by with her cart, and sitting in the smoking car afterward, exhaling long purple plumes as I looked out on the rice fields and clouds. Going to the theater and walking in the Ginza afterward. Viewing irises at the Imperial Palace, taking a rowboat out to paddle underneath its blossoming cherry trees in spring. These were all hewn from some larger myth or daydream. They were girlish fantasies.

The erotic was not sexual but filled with the promise of sex, the trappings of it, the context in which it bloomed and fired, the moment before, or after. It was *suggestion*. Erotic puns appeared in our music, like *nurete*, a word that meant "wet" to describe the streets on a rainy night in the pleasure quarters. Ears were erotic, hidden as they were under a cape of hair. The nape of the neck. The hint of a hot red underrobe under a geisha's black robe.

Sensei used Edo language like *yoi no kuchi*, the night is young, when we were practicing late into the night, or *murasaki* instead of *shoyu*, for soy sauce, at a meal. She was joking. She didn't really live in Edo. But it stood for some kind of sophistication or dignity. An apartness that was vital to her music.

So much seemed to be hidden.

"If you have no secrets," wrote the novelist Kawabata Yasunari, "you are not living your own life."

=

The Edo-Tokyo Museum, the site of our concert, sat tucked behind the Sumo Stadium in Ryogoku, a flat plain to the east across the Sumida River, where ferries once shuttled pleasure-seekers to the Yoshiwara red-light district upstream. The museum was also an earthquake shelter. Sensei was pleased at the thought that, in the event of disaster that afternoon, modern Tokyo might crumble around us but the instruments would be saved.

We arrived mid-morning, carrying them protectively under umbrellas in an early spring drizzle, watching out for puddles in our snow-white tabi. Sensei wore a pair of *geta* clogs with little plastic windshields. The museum was near the sumo stadium. Wrestlers teetered by on bicycles, like fairytale giants, nearly tipping as they turned to watch our clutch of foreigners in kimono hurried past.

We set up in a conference room with long tables that served as a green room. There was the feeling of two camps. Across from us, the Queen's students, young Japanese men and women, were assembling their instruments and talking together.

"Kuki ga warui, ne," Sensei said, describing the atmosphere as "out of tune."

There was no joshing or good-natured comparing of shamisen, no questions about country of origin or language. If we'd run into one of these students on a train platform, lost in Shibuya, they would have surely guided us, as so many did, trying out their English along the way. But here we were intruders. The intimacies of the ancient music had no place in the present.

The students were changing their strings.

"Not smart," Sensei said. "They will stretch in performance. Big problem."

Sensei introduced Kenneth to the Queen, whom I recognized right away as the tall woman in an emerald kimono with brittle features and thick eye makeup who was waving her jeweled fingers at people as if sweeping them out of corners. Girls in pastel kimono trailed her with envelopes of money.

Sensei told the Queen about Kenneth's dissertation. He had changed his topic to *nagauta*, the "long songs" that were the style Sensei taught.

"Did you know?" she asked me.

Of course I didn't know.

The Queen took new interest in Kenneth, and perhaps Sensei, too.

Denise and I went to 7-Eleven for snacks. Doug tried to make conversation in Japanese. Lena was dressed like the men, in black slacks and white shirt. Sensei worried about Doug's shirt staying white or forgetting his *yubikake,* the crucial finger sling. From time to time she glided over to me in the green room and tugged my collar closed. "Too sexy."

Denise had helped me pick out my first kimono. "Get *araeru*," Sensei advised. "Washable," meaning polyester. Even so, it was lovely: a muted green with pale pink cherry blossoms. The pattern was a little youthful for my age—late twenties—and the kimono narrow. "Enormous," Sensei had said, tugging the robe around my legs as she dressed me that morning. Finally, she'd secured the robe closed with garters and clips that chafed all day.

With more time to spare, the group wandered into the museum, where we walked over a life-sized reproduction of the Nihonbashi Bridge and peered in at a miniature Minami-za, a famous kabuki theater in Edo. I recognized hair combs, books sewn up the right side, and other objects from Sensei's rooms.

When the West came, in the Meiji period, Edo changed to Tokyo, "Eastern Capital," and the city was refashioned with industry, trains, Western paintings, and Victorian dresses. The campaign to modernize was called "Civilization and Enlightenment." The plentiful fires of Edo continued, along with the Great Kanto Earthquake in 1923, after each of which the city again rebuilt, and again after the Tokyo fire bombings of 1945, in which more people were killed than in Hiroshima and Nagasaki combined. I still couldn't figure out how the U.S. and Japan had gotten past that. Photos showed postwar GIs handing out chocolate bars and chewing gum to Japanese people smiling in defeat. And how did I not know anything about this culture, which had been so deeply entwined with my own?

The exhibit would disabuse me of any rescue fantasies. Japan kept moving on, renewing, modernizing, persisting. I passed construction zones daily where old buildings came down in no time, and new ones were erected alarmingly fast. I sometimes feared that an earthquake would destroy all the old things I loved and they would never be rebuilt: the *tenugui* cloth shop in Asakusa, the tabi seller in Ginza, the three-hundred-year-old incense shop.

These thoughts now seem, if not foolish, then only partially aware. The Japanese, if anything, thrive on contrast: the silence of a shrine next to booming video towers, the kabuki theater next to Broadway musicals. The contrast was what was interesting.

Is this why Sensei had stressed, from the beginning, *ma,* space? It was a musical construct, an idea, but it also seemed a signal to allow for other forces at play. A rescue is clear, unequivocal. Someone is drowning, you pull them to shore. The space seemed to imply, "You are not master here. Something else is in control."

The more I tried to pin anything down, to define it once and for all, the more it eluded me. Sensei included.

=

The shamisen was slipperier in kimono. I used two sticky lap pads to keep it in place, balancing it carefully while I turned the pages of my score. The university students had memorized the song like professionals. I tried hard to follow the tempo, which seemed fast. I heard someone play a note in a space of *ma.* Someone's shamisen was already out of tune.

The tempo accelerated and I tried to slow down the tempo by playing behind the beat, but to no effect. The song got faster until the *chirashi* exploded, the spaces hardly audible in the din of instruments and drum calls. Finally, I saw the automatic curtain begin to move across the stage. The last note in our music was never seen, only heard. My finger hovered over the last position as I waited for the final cue. Drummers' hands were outstretched, their voices puttied howls, *"Iyaaaa!"* The flute pealed, *"Hiiiiii!"* We were alive, in one long buzzing frenzy, like a giant insect, everyone arrived to this place, together, this height above the abyss, waiting for the cue, finally, to finish.

Backstage afterward, the Japanese students moved the desks into a horseshoe and a young man in kimono started passing hors d'oeuvres and cups of white wine. I was just reaching for one when Sensei touched my elbow. "We are leaving."

I bowed at the boy and gathered my things. Sensei said that the Queen was now going to tell them all their mistakes. It was a typical post-concert wrap.

No one mentioned our going, and it seemed as if they'd hardly noticed we were there in the first place.

"I had thought that we might talk to the students about shamisen," I said to Sensei on the train.

"Of course not," she said. "Japanese music has nothing to do with Japanese culture." As I started to protest, she shook her head. "Totally different." She raised her chin and realigned the sharp cut of her hair at her jaw. "I knew," she said quietly.

≡

When Sensei lit a candle at the kitchen table during a late-night snack after long hours of music, I knew its arrival meant we were leaving ordinary time. It was an attempt to keep the hush, the mystery, and cloaked companionship of the music room with us a little longer before returning to our lives. The idea was born that night after the March concert. Call it an after-party, a post-stage bash. Unlike the properly organized ritual of the Queen, this was a complete unstringing of the day. Sensei named it a "candle party."

We lowered the music table and loaded it with plates of sushi, crinkle-cut French fries, burdock root salad, fried chicken, and dumplings. Tiny cans of Asahi beer were cracked, including one plum spritzer for Sensei, and the bottle of Johnny Walker Red was brought down from its place atop the fridge. We stashed the instruments in the corner of the music room. Piles of washable kimono were already churning in the washer. Sensei's tabi were in the sink, awaiting scrubbing of their finely herringboned soles. In her steel square bathtub sat our backpacks, and by the door, lined up on newspapers, our shoes.

When Sensei's rooms were full like this it was chaos. Four standing gaijin in her kitchen seemed to fill it completely, replacing the cracking concrete corners, the dimness, the faded linoleum with colorful sweaters, lipstick, hairdos, smiles, and jokes. The sad insistencies of the music, the still pauses that gave shape to its sounds, shattered.

"Come on there. Easy does it," Alan teased Sensei. "You don't want to look like Konishiki, the sumo wrestler!"

Sensei patted her tummy. "So fat."

Her neck tilted coquettishly, and reddened. Alcohol worked on her quickly.

"*Kanpai!* Cheers!"

"Gaijin take Japan!"

"Here's to Sensei!"

"Marriage is shit!" she called out. She made an "O" with her mouth. Kenneth's marriage in the States was faltering in his absence, we'd heard. I knew him little but through music at Sensei's.

Soon we settled in around the question of what happened in the performance. What went wrong? For something had. We were thrilled. The *drama* of it. And it wasn't one of us.

That final note of the song had never arrived.

The lead shamisen player's opening *kakegoe* was too fast, Sensei explained, now back in teacherly mode.

Kakegoe was literally "the hanging voice," a tiny syllable—*yo, ho, iya*—used to keep the whole orchestra intact. That breath of air—"*Yo!*"—to start the orchestra, well, it was just a syllable but the way it was said was a cue to tempo. This was the wildly improvisational counterpoint to exquisitely repeated *kata.* The one allowance for spontaneity that made each performance unique, never to be repeated.

Too much gusto, that was the issue. Her *yo* was too fast, which is why we were careening through the song. At the end, it wasn't forceful enough, which is why no one heard it and we couldn't arrive together at the end.

I was fascinated by the consequence of a tiny moment of sound. Who knew? Maybe the girl had the hiccoughs.

"How about *o-shami*?" Sensei said. Someone handed her an instrument and she began strumming with her fingernails. "*Harukaze ga soyo soyo to …*" "The spring wind whispers …" She translated as she sang. "The courtesan is tempting her lover to stay with her under the quilts drinking hot ginger sake, snow outside …" The contrast of hot and cold was supposed to be vivifying, arousing.

Sensei clinked glasses with Kenneth. She asked Alan to fill her glass, to which she toasted, "All just live together!"

I chewed a dumpling and tried to smile.

It occurs to me now that learning the shamisen and a music that could never be mine is like being doomed to perpetually unrequited love. Which means, I suppose, that I was learning something about desire and yearning after all.

The shamisen's slender and elegant art endured. People were playing it strenuously, devotedly, in their own way. And this was a great disappointment.

How many times had Sensei stood at a distance when dressing me in kimono and said, of the colors and patterns, "No, too sad" or "Too warm?" Contrast was the goal, a combination that surprised.

The traits Sensei and I clashed on were the ones that drew us together: independence and single-minded focus, and when those dipped out of sight, as they did now, I didn't understand.

Around ten, she pulled the string to the overhead light and said the candle party was over. We began to clear the plates. Sensei washed, someone dried, another put the cups and plates away in her hutch. Backpacks were collected from where they were stashed in the tub and shoes laced and tied at the door.

I stayed a long time, fussing with my shoes slowly.

"Do you need some food, Janet? Are you ok? Some tea?"

A woman in kimono had secret places: the lip of the obi, the throat of the sleeve, the sliver of collar folded left over right. In these places she could conceal things—a fan, a house key, envelopes of money—and carry them effortlessly along, hidden.

A woman who is *iki* did the same thing. To be *iki*, a woman has to have been around a bit and have tasted the bitterness, as well as the sweetness, of love. Young girls seldom had this quality; it was the women approaching middle age who could be *iki*. *Iki* was not one-dimensional, literal, seeking consummation. This was the main difference between Sensei and me. I strove to protect her, tiny and delicate, and the disappearing gentle sounds of Japan, but could never match her sophistication, her Japaneseness. In the end, I was too innocent.

8

… a near primitive instinct took hold of me …

Sensei's solution to despair was beauty, and it sat in a wedge of hallway between the music room and the bath in the form of a tall orange lacquer chest with black fastenings. On it sat her fax machine, where she sent her music ad out into the world. The fax was covered with a light cotton hand towel, for dust, and I think, for its design: an image of a young girl in kimono gazing at a goldfish in a bowl.

Sensei bought the chest before starting her life teaching music to foreigners. She was feeling low, very low, as in, "Should I keep going?" she told me one evening when we were eating quietly after a lesson. "I wanted to kill myself," was how she put it, actually.

I had felt low, too, had asked myself this question once or twice—hasn't every thinking person? For years I used to slowly edge close to a pillar and take hold when the subway whooshed past in Boston or New York, less because I wanted to jump but for fear that my body, knowing something I did not, would act without me.

Suicide was a reality in Japanese life. Corrupt politicians and corporate presidents committed honorable suicide rather than bring disgrace to their families with their crimes. Lovers jumped into the cone of Mount Fuji. Students who failed to get into universities and foresaw only a life of shameful toil outside the system would wire themselves to an alarm clock to be electrocuted on awakening. "Jumpers" were the reasons the trains in Tokyo sometimes stopped and begged our patience while staff attended to a matter on the tracks.

I don't know all the details of that time, but what struck me about Sensei was that, in such a low place, she could organize herself enough to board a bullet train to Kyoto to look for antiques at her favorite store, Gomokudo, in Gion, an old geisha district. She greeted the elegant proprietress there, sipped a cup of tea, and negotiated a purchase. I would not be surprised if money was not even exchanged, wired later perhaps, so they could focus on the atmosphere, the transference of the object from one individual to the next, the ritual pouring of hot water over tea leaves, the conversation about life, art, Kyoto.

Once, when I was making a trip to Kyoto, Sensei asked me to visit this woman. "You will know why when you see her."

The shop was in a tiny back street. I had asked my host if we could make a stop there, I would be brief. I had with me a video of Sensei's latest concert, to give to the proprietress. When I entered, a woman in a pale yellow silk kimono approached. She contained a gentleness and refinement I could barely describe, only inhale in her presence. It calmed and soothed. She was an atmosphere all her own.

When I introduced myself, thanking her on Sensei's behalf and presenting her with the packages, she got a faraway look. "Ah …," she said, and murmured Sensei's name. I understood completely. The woman gave me hope. Not only that something ancient and refined was alive and well, or that one could fold oneself into beauty. But that one could learn to efface oneself and not disappear.

=

Sensei and I never openly disagreed. The Japanese never did. I had to intuit displeasure or disapproval. It was through things she didn't say that I would sometimes learn her true feelings.

I worried about our bond. Our relationship was provisional, imbalanced, always shifting. I didn't know which students would be there in the evenings, what pieces I would be learning next, what performances were to come. I needed to nail something down, to have some sliver of control over what I was learning. To seduce something of my own. And so, that spring, after the concert at the museum, my second in Japan, I seduced Yoshi.

I had no female friends in Tokyo at the time. Amy, my friend from college, had moved and we'd lost touch. The Japanese students at my new school were a self-selected breed of exiles. After our two-year course, they were guaranteed acceptance at one of a dozen schools in the U.S. They were not stellar students and didn't seem to have any particular motivation for international studies. They liked to use American words for idealized situations. *Doraibu*, "drive," instead of *unten*, called up a dreamy Sunday drive along the coast with a lover. *Deeto*, "date," had a special intrigue that only the nglicized version could express. They may have been with us because they couldn't fit in anywhere else. They'd gotten off track in school and were now what are called *ronin*, masterless samurai.

Chris, a teacher from New York in the cubicle next to me, circled all their errors gleefully in red. "They'll learn one way or the other!" he boomed. I wrote encouraging notes and squeezed in extra points so they wouldn't give up. Chris and I took the same train, and sometimes stopped to have a beer at Standee, a bar on the train platform, his input, at least double mine, instigating a slight stagger as we pushed into the crammed cars.

Sensei became my new friend and confidante. I didn't need any other friends, and I saved my stories for her kitchen table on music breaks. After a long afternoon of music on a weekend, when our meal could be more luxurious, she might send me out to Shinanoya, an international grocer next to the apartment she had secured for Kenneth, for creamy pumpkin salad, baby cheeses, skewers of chicken and asparagus, batter-fried eggplant, to which she would add the staples of rice, soup, and pickles. I looked forward to these meals, which had a festive feel, and I knew we could talk longer, uncork new topics to explore.

I lingered after weekday sessions, when, after two or three students in a row, she stopped at 9 p.m. to start her ablutions: a shower (she never seemed to use her bath), and the methodical preening of her hair. On a little chair in front of a mirror, she watched dubbed episodes of *Beverly Hills, 90210*—"It's trash!" I told her; "Interesting," she said—as she went through the same series of actions each night, as repeatable as inserting the bridge under the shamisen's strings. Head tilted, she drew the dryer brush down the length of each patch of strands, extending them out as far and as straight as they would go, then dropped them and slid her hand along the edge at her neck, depositing loose hairs in a tiny pail at her feet.

Hair assembled, she then patted her cheeks with shark fin oil using the palms of her hands. She squatted on the threshold between bath and kitchen and brushed her teeth while I finally laced up my shoes in the *genkan*. She was in her pajamas by then, traditional men's PJs with the breast pocket and white piping at the wrist, probably in the size for a young boy. It was a mystery how the hair remained intact through sleep.

I never heard her speak of friends or going to have a coffee with so-and-so. *I don't want to waste my time.* She was single-minded in her focus on music, as if she'd been given an expiry date on her life and had to get things done by then.

I spoke rarely of Sensei. I didn't have anyone to share her with or speak of her to. And so her words and notes went deep inside me and rarely surfaced.

Was she a cult? I have sometimes wondered. She certainly had power, as I had seen at the candle party, shimmering in her own pool, attracting everyone to her shores. But it was a soft power, a power that came playfully and as a way to entertain the students.

No, if anything, for me, it was her power over herself that intrigued. The person who could turn on the lights at ten o'clock and break up the party, the part of her who could, after a performance, say, "It's over." She knew how to be on her own. I didn't.

Sometimes, when recapping a moment or reflecting on some action she had taken or not taken, she would say, "I hardly know myself."

I would get angry then, because she could look at herself as a specimen under glass, and I could not. "Yes you do," I wanted to say. It was her surety of un-surety, her complete acceptance of it that made me want to contradict her.

One day on the train going somewhere, she asked, "How do you know yourself?"

"I don't know," I said. "I write in my journal."

"Works?" She turned her eyes to me.

"Yeah, I guess so."

"Very hard, life," she said. "We can't see ourselves. Like some fog in our eyes. We can't know our thinking. We just have to do and then we find out. But too late. Kind of wrong order. Life is very ironic, Janet."

≡

It made sense to align with Japanese culture. What I was learning—music—was at its core, its *kokoro*, despite what Sensei said. The truth was, I did not know where the music resided in my life exactly, or where Sensei did, either. I couldn't define our relationship. It was so unlike anything else I'd experienced. And more powerful, too. I depended on her for so much, and it shamed me.

Yoshi brought me to all the places I wanted to go outside Sensei's rooms. Bookstores, music shops, curry restaurants, department stores. He took me to the diner where the writer Natsume Soseki ate breakfast, the bar where Dazai Osamu drank. When the plums blossomed in February we went to a park to view them. They were best viewed up close, he said, while cherries were best seen from far away. He took pictures of me avidly, not as an expert photographer, but a chronicler. He gave them to me later, like Sensei who handed me a plastic baggie of photos with my name written on it in her disconnected cursive hand. I looked more natural in the pictures at Sensei's.

"Roba-chan," Yoshi called me, making a pun of the last syllable of my name, *roba*, which meant "donkey" in Japanese. He goaded me to buy things with my lavish English teacher's salary and then carried my packages on the streets. He came to a kimono fashion show I was in outside a department store in Shinjuku. I can't remember who invited me to model. It was a stormy day, pouring rain, and I'd spent the day with other foreigners from around the world, getting our hair twisted into exotic shapes, and our nails lacquered. During the show, Yoshi stood under a tree, snapping away: me winking at him from the catwalk, a close-up of my manicured toes. He was soaked.

Yoshi brought me into *izakaya,* cozy local bars with no plastic food displays outside, where we curled up on cushions and drank sake from square pine boxes salted in the corners. Sensei never went into pubs or department stores. She rarely went out. Food was delivered from her co-op, just the basics that she needed, some vegetables and fish to add to miso and rice. Dining out beyond Gusto next door, which we used as our personal commissary when music rehearsals squeezed out time for food, was a waste of time.

I was obsessed with Yoshi's hair. Wavy, inky curls, it looked shiny and soft but when I touched it, the strands were thick, almost coarse. I wrapped curls around my fingers as we lay on the futon, watching TV. I studied the triangle of his jaw, his cheekbones, the tiny space of his upper lip.

Mine was the first shamisen he'd seen. He made jokes about skinning a cat when a stray one crossed our path in Tokyo. When I told him about Sensei, he listened across the *kotatsu* in my apartment after cooking us meals of eggy *omuraisu* or rolled cabbage leaves, a chopstick in my Obunsha dictionary between us.

"But gaijin will leave, *ne?*"

"So they'll take it with them and teach others. And besides, not all leave. I'm here, no?"

I loved most our afternoons at Renoir, a cafe where we sat in high-backed green velvet chairs and sipped coffee from china cups. It was gone in two sips but they let us linger long after, me doodling kanji and onomatopoeia in my notebook: *hoka hoka,* "piping hot"; *pika pika,* "squeaky clean"; *shito shito,* "falling rain."

Sensei's rooms contained all that was necessary. When I came to her one day with a new set of shamisen strings, she asked, "W—hy?" We had Kameya, the family of shamisen makers she patronized who could supply anything we needed. When leaving Gusto and I bought a funny cigarette lighter or change purse, she asked, "Do you need?" and squinted up at me. "No meaning."

I had stopped wearing jewelry because I had to remove it all when playing the shamisen. I wore no makeup, preferring a natural style. I lived in one room that served all my needs, rolling out bedding at night and restoring it to the futon closet in the morning. I boiled hot water to do dishes and bathe, washed clothes by transferring them from washer to wringer and hanging them out to dry. Living within limits was a challenge, but battering human instinct with the force of will was necessary.

Yoshi, who lived in Adachi-ku, near Ueno, the old part of Tokyo, was the first thing I did outside of Sensei and it felt daring. A former student of mine in Odawara (how else to meet someone?), he was as lonely and broody as I was, and eight years younger. His father was head of an old department store. His mother had died when he was sixteen and he had spent a year out of school grieving and cutting himself.

But after he returned to school he never quite adjusted. Out of synch with his peers, he was full of dreams of escape, of a desire to leave Japan, and of a kind of rage at the unfairness of life. He liked the word "fuck," and said it whenever he could. "Fuck fuck fuck fuck fuck."

Sensei knew I was seeing him. "Date with Yoshi?" she said, when I left her rooms early on a Saturday night.

I didn't offer details. More than once, Sensei, at the sink washing the dishes after a lesson, had mused, "Love or music? Which one do you choose?"

If I said "love," I feared she'd think me shallow. If I said, "music," I feared she'd think me a fool. It was clear by now that Kenneth was her favorite. After the museum concert, Sensei started taking Kenneth to her teacher for singing lessons. She took him to her flute lessons, too, and interviews with musicians, concerts he mustn't miss. I pictured them out in Tokyo, Kenneth under his heavy backpack, Sensei's sandal straps slung off her heels. In her rooms, she started taking down from her shelves a green leather bound book to explain the music to Kenneth and translate its words. It seemed a sorting out had taken place, some decision I wasn't aware of.

To her own question Sensei answered, "I choose music. More stable life."

But she didn't look down on love. If anything, she respected its pull and power. Once, I came into a lesson startled and more than a little excited to see a couple in a screaming match in front of her building." Sensei had shuddered, as if visibly soiled by the image. "I don't want to lose control."

One day in the English newspaper there was an article titled, "Shamisensuality," written by a middle-aged Japanese man who confessed he had never heard the shamisen. Reviewing a concert, he described the shamisen's "erotic charm," its "ability to fan the embers of desire." "Honestly speaking," he wrote, "I felt myself becoming sexually aroused."

"How dumb!" I said to Sensei. "It's not about sex. What a jerk."

She shook her head. "So sad, he doesn't know his own culture."

We resumed our talk of the music's subtlety and grace, its refinement and poise.

I don't know who we were kidding.

Love was in the air all the time, in the music, the songs, the stories. It was the root of all trouble, celebrated most when doomed. Unrequited disasters infused the music with a sad sweetness that throbbed. If love was impossible, it was also unsullied, pure.

Love in Sensei's life didn't seem to have any fixed object. There was her music, a subject of serious study, and there was Kenneth, who was a part of her passion and purpose.

She kept mini Asahi beers in the fridge for him. She fed all of us, but only for Kenneth did she keep the little silver cans knotted together in plastic loops. Kenneth was always on her mind—a new song he could learn, the sound of his flute, his excellent voice. She often talked about music being "pure." Freeing it from the shackles of tradition would give it a value of its own. At group lessons, she let him help tune the shamisen and sing *Kurokami*, a song about a geisha who waits so long for her jilting lover to return that her hair turns as white as the snow at the end of the song. By the end of the first line of notes, my feet were asleep.

If Sensei seduced, I reasoned, it was not for selfish reasons but because she had to. She needed music to survive, to orient her to the world. I do not believe she would have survived without it. She would have been a bag lady under a bridge in Shinjuku. Or perhaps just a lonely woman in Toyama wandering the streets, like the old women from Edo in her childhood, with their outdated, impossible hairstyles.

Watching students arrive and then leave, betray her, abandon her, and disappoint her made me promise to myself that I would never do any of those things. A promise that, of course, I could never keep.

=

Sometimes Yoshi and I went to love hotels, where I had heard single women were not allowed to enter—as some did for a respite from chores and children—because too many had ended up hanging themselves by the bed sheets. The buildings were nondescript but for a sign outside, Rest ¥3,000, Stay ¥7,000. When we went in Yoshi always planted me in a corner while he approached the clerk behind a plexiglass window, sliding through the small opening several large flat bills. You would not know Yoshi had money except for this endless stream of bills, the expensive watch swimming on his wrist, the designer sneakers. The jeans were old, the sweater worn, the hair only occasionally washed. Upstairs in the carpeted and mirrored rooms, after polite conversation and tea in the "conversation corner," and a thorough scrubbing of my elbows and knees in the shower, we made love like a Kawabata novel: a plotless accumulation of gestures and then a silent falling away.

Yoshi was a replacement for the intimacy I wanted with Sensei, the old one-on-one hunger and conversation like we'd had early on, at the kitchen table, two women finding their purpose in life. Part of love was being Other, singular, with no one else in the picture, and I was hoping that through Yoshi, Sensei might see that I was adored, wanted by someone. She was with Kenneth doing very great things, things I would never be a part of.

Sensei's rooms enveloped me with the slow sad strings, the legends and histories settling over my shoulders like an ancient shawl. Yoshi was bullet trains to Kyoto. Tokyo Disneyland. Drinks and dinners at those cozy *izakaya*. Linked with Yoshi, people looked at me differently. I would sometimes catch a glimpse of myself in a store window and be shocked to see round eyes and brown wavy hair. I was viewed as a gaijin who understood Japan. A woman who *knew*, and that in itself was erotic. Everything I was learning with Yoshi made up for everything I could never know with Sensei. It was like smuggling money from one bank account into another.

I was ripe for Yoshi's teachings. When he protested the opinionated buttons on my denim jacket—*Books not Bombs, AIDS in the ESOL Classroom*—I took them off. When he got angry at a loose bra I was wearing, visible through an armhole in my sleeveless shirt, I sat mutely while he stitched the gap closed.

But I often got it wrong. Once, Yoshi offered to pick up my bicycle at the train station. I said yes. "No, no," he said. "You have to say no many times before you say yes. This is *enryo*, restraint." I spoke too loudly on the train, and laughed without covering my mouth— bared teeth were aggressive. Once when we were going to find an Edo-period garden in the center of the city I began to flip through my Lonely Planet guidebook as we walked. Yoshi brooded and fell several steps behind.

"What's wrong?" I asked.

He could barely contain his anger. "Why do you need me?" he asked

I said something, he said something, we didn't seem to understand each other. It wasn't language, it was motive, intent, deeper meanings that the language failed us in rendering. Finally, I understood that he was referring to the guidebook. It was selfish to take care of my own needs instead of depending on him. I put it away and took his arm.

When a snarl like this occurred when we were out, Yoshi would sometimes steer me into a café and order American blends so we could consult our dictionaries. Finally, when we'd exhausted all possible words and I'd have a splitting headache, we would exit the café, the tangle approached if not resolved, and walk on until we could speak again. Sometimes we rented a room in a love hotel to try to reach further approximations there.

A near primitive instinct took hold of me to belong and fit in, as the Japanese had all this time, locked onto their long spiny islands with no resources and too many people. And so these disagreements—though they weren't even that, more like potential disagreements that would only blossom if we could figure out what the other meant—were like knots in your hair, impenetrable and only loosened with great caution and patience.

So I tried to make a show of my gratitude at all times. On a trip to Kyoto I paid to get dressed up as a maiko, apprentice geisha. I flitted through the photo shoot: pretending to play a *koto*, fake-performing a tea ceremony. Back on the street after I'd washed off the white greasepaint from my hands and neck, I raved about the experience. I thought it would make him feel glad, since he had loaned me some money for the extra features. He had sponsored my enjoyment.

Yoshi sulked all the way back to the inn. I asked what was wrong.

"I gave you money. It's okay. I had money. I gave to you. But you don't thank me."

"But I did! I thanked you when you gave it to me."

"You keep talking about it and you don't say I gave it to you."

The transaction had connected us in some way I did not understand. All I knew was that to now equate the event with his charity made it feel like the experience was no longer mine.

I could see what Sensei said sometimes: "Japan only cares about the 'container,' not inside." But it was important to me to do things right, so part of my nature then, and the belief that if I could, some new and improved self would appear.

I wonder now if these tangles, too, were stand-ins for tangles with Sensei. *The two lines—shamisen and voice—must never meet*. If we couldn't be in conflict, how could we understand each other? The instructions, the love hotels, all of it felt vindicating.

One day on the train, during some kind of outburst, Yoshi

slapped me across the face. After several minutes, I quietly told him to never do that again.

I felt I had to be an insider to earn Sensei's favor and trust, to encourage her to say, "Ah, you will stay, you win the prize, here are all my secrets...."

Perhaps it is I who, at the time, needed a secret.

≡

One night we ran into Sensei on the overpass over Lucky Seven Boulevard. When I spotted her figure coming down the stairs I froze. She stopped in her tracks and ran a hand along her hair. Cars zoomed below on the street.

I overdid my surprise. "Where are you going?" I nearly shouted. I could never be casual with Sensei and it felt foolish to try now. My shopping bags wilted in my hands: Italian sandals and a Roland keyboard so Yoshi could learn to play "Yesterday" by the Beatles.

"I just came from shamisen lesson," she said, intoning insistently the syllables *less-on*.

I introduced Yoshi, who bowed and mumbled a string of syllables. Sensei nodded and closed her collar around her neck.

"Looks conservative," she said at my next lesson.

"Oh, not at all," I said. I told her how he hated the emperor and flipped off the Imperial Palace.

I have always felt that Sensei's transformation—becoming more American, that is, breezier, sexier, wittier—was more fun. Mine was harder going. With Yoshi I was becoming zipped up, pressed-lip, elbows-in proper, and failing badly.

Whether to point all this out to me, or as an act of finally accepting the relationship and bringing us all together, she suggested we attend together the highly dramatic, artificial dream dance of the kabuki. She would buy the tickets.

Since Sensei never voluntarily left the music, the kabuki was perhaps a natural choice. The kabuki was her world. And we would not have to interact much. It was like going on a first date to a movie.

Yoshi showed up at the station in Ginza in a three-piece suit of gray pinstriped wool with a high-buttoned vest. With his little wire-rim spectacles and thick black hair, he looked like a handsome visitor from a Nagai Kafu novel of the 1920s.

"Do you like it?" he asked on a backstreet corner near the Kabuki-za, stopping me with a propped leg on a window sill. He looked at me, then down to his buttery leather ankle boot. His ensemble must have cost a fortune and was probably from his Adults' Day Ceremony a few months earlier, when he'd turned twenty.

"Nice," I said, touching the toe of his boot so we could move on.

Sensei was waiting in the red-carpeted lobby of the theater with a dramatic scarf tied around her neck. In the crook of her elbow, her tote brimmed with scores, dictionaries, and a bamboo flute. As soon as I saw her I fell onto her arm.

Yoshi and Sensei greeted each other in Japanese, with no more interest or familiarity than on the street the previous week. People were pressing past with earphone guides and lunch boxes. The bittersweet smell of incense crowded the air.

"We should go up?" Sensei said to me in English. She asked Yoshi on the stairs if he had been to the kabuki before. *"Hajimete desu,"* he said. "It's my first time." His whole body was thrown forward from the shoulders, like a football player holding an infant.

"Many versions. This is Rokusaburo's *Renjishi,* from around 1819. The music is a little different from Katsusaburo's, which is more common to hear," she said in English.

"So desu ka?" Yoshi chimed in.

We settled into the front row of the third-floor balcony. As drums began to boom, Sensei pointed. Diagonal to stage right, Denise was draped over the railing, staring down at the *hanamichi.* What a coincidence, I said. "I knew," was her reply.

The first play was a *jidaimono,* a stylized play with lots of hand wringing, grotesque leers, and gorgeous costumes. Sensei wore her big clunky eyeglasses and passed us her binoculars. She tapped drum beats on her lap and consulted a score in her bag. Yoshi sat with his hands between his legs. He seemed conservative and callow now. What happened to the smoldering handholding, the hours of flirting in cafes? Sensei was scanning the musicians now, leaning in to whisper a bit of knowledge or gossip. I didn't want to miss some new learning, or "listening" as I was beginning to think of her tips.

"I was waiting for that!" yelled someone from the rear.

At the intermission, we found Denise in the lobby. Up next was *Renjishi*, a famous lion dance. Denise had danced it years ago. It is the story of a papa lion and his cub, who must trudge the long road to independence by surviving being kicked off a cliff and left to scramble up on his own.

"Tough love," Sensei piped up. I nodded, and looked at Yoshi.

The buzzer sounded and we filed back to our seats. I smiled at Yoshi on the stairs but he said nothing. "Why aren't you talking?" I whispered. "I can't speak English!" he said. "Yes, you can!" "No I can't!" "What are you talking about?" I said. "You speak it fine."

The curtain opened again and the dance began. The cub was being played by the real-life son of the father lion. Sensei scanned the musicians with her binoculars. Yoshi clasped his hands, as if awaiting some kind of punishment.

As the papa waited for the cub to scramble back up, the musicians went silent. The actor leered, flailed desperately, and finally struck a *mie* pose, crossing one eye to wild applause. The music stretched like putty into thick silences between drumbeats. The drummer's roar rose in pitch. "*Yooo-hoooooo!*" There was a pause. One beat. Two. Then the soft tap-tap of the stick *taiko*. There seemed no order to the silences or the beats, as if only wild improvisation could express the madness of grief. I counted thirty-two beats, then sixteen, then eight, then all three drums and a flute were playing wildly and the two actors scampered onstage as lions, wigs waving, leaping with peonies and butterflies.

At the next intermission, Denise talked about how hard it was to cross one eye in a *mie*. "How did the drums know to come in like that? Their timing was perfect!" I asked Sensei. "Kind of counting system for drum. I can teach you," she said and checked her watch. She had to get up early for a Sunday student. She and Yoshi exchanged bows, he a low one, she a little head nod, and she turned and walked down the red-carpeted lobby stairs slightly sideways, as if wearing a kimono instead of slacks.

Yoshi and I returned to our seats. The final drama was a historical play. The set was in drab indigos and tans, the only music a plinking off-stage shamisen to punctuate the dialogue. We sat not touching or talking until Yoshi suddenly got up and walked out mid-performance. I followed him down three flights of stairs and out the heavy doors, where I found him walking in the direction of Tsukiji, the all-night fish market friends would go to after partying to have sushi for breakfast.

He stopped on a pedestrian bridge over the Sumida River. The Sumida was everywhere in our music. It was the river that ferried people around in Edo, when boats were the main transportation. At our backs was Ginza, where my students window-shopped hopefully, and where I bought kimono, tabi, and other ancient accessories with Sensei.

What was she doing right now? I wondered. Even her hair-drying ritual felt more vital to me than what Yoshi and I were doing on any given day. While I was browsing postcards at flea markets or sampling sushi flavors, she was home placing another student's hands on the shamisen, showing them how to sharpen the tuning without stripping the delicate sandalwood pegs. I had gotten that right away, as I did washing my hands before touching the instrument, which Sensei said had told her I was a true musician.

Why had I stayed here, if not to learn something important? Something I felt would transform me and take me to a different kind of life?

When I arrived at my lesson the next week, Sensei didn't pre-amble with tea or chat in the kitchen but led us directly to the music table. Laid out were two shamisen, like head-to-toe sleeping siblings. She dropped a score covered in pink washi paper on the table in front of me.

I recognized the kanji.

"*Renjishi!*" I said.

"Very masculine piece," she said. "Flashy. You will like."

I do not know whether she had been sensing my boredom, seeing my skill all along, or if this was another lesson about focusing on what was important, but I took it as the official word that I was getting somewhere. I was worthy of more secrets and techniques. *Hijiriki*, a fluttering of the fingers backward over the strings. Pizzicato, a quick plucking of the pick. It took hours to slog through the whole forty-minute piece. Sensei had decided on the next performance in August. We had to be ready.

In the kitchen after, she clicked off the overhead light and brought a small votive candle to the table. "Cozy," she said. "Our own candle party." She slipped into her apron, keys jangling in the pocket, and began her kitchen music: opening the fridge, lighting the burner for tea, and popping two packets of red rice, usually reserved for celebrations, into the microwave.

I sipped the six-ounce beer she brought me. One of Kenneth's? She sipped her plum spritzer and began telling me a story. Instead of dreamy ruminations about a future concert or a student's talents, this was another piece of the past that unraveled between the night's music.

"I was working in the tropical fish corner at a department store …," she began.

It was the early 1970s. Sensei was twenty-three or twenty-four and still new to Tokyo. I could not imagine her without her musical mission with foreigners. Her rebelliousness had not yet been finely tuned; it was still bubbling under the surface. But she probably walked the same way, one foot in front of the other, a little proud, believing she was different from the rest.

A German student at Rikyo University, who worked at the American military base, used to come in every day with his interpreter to talk to Sensei. "He had a crush on me," she said. "The Allied troops were still all around Tokyo. Foreigners were not human being back then. He said I was 'pretty.' I didn't know the word yet."

The microwave beeped and she put in the second package of rice and pressed the button. Her microwave didn't need a timer setting. It automatically stopped when the food was heated through. I called it her Miracle Wave.

"He invited me to the base. So I dressed in kimono and we had dinner there. He was thirty-six or thirty-seven. He wanted to marry me."

He proposed to Sensei through an interpreter.

"But how could you have communicated?"

"I could learn," she said, as if learning English was something she could pick up like a quart of milk on the way home. And indeed, she seemed to have. Her English was not fluent but never seemed incomplete. She always got her meaning across. With Yoshi there were many things I still could not understand, even as my Japanese improved.

"Anyway, no language problem," she said. "Spirit and heart are more important."

She was right. Music had nothing to do with culture, with Japan even. It was a bond stronger than culture or family or blood, and she and I were inside it, drawn together by an invisible fourth string that hovered over the shamisen's three.

She took a sip of spritzer.

"So what happened?" I asked.

"I was tempted, but I broke up with him. Before we, you know … That could have been my life."

Why that story then? I have wondered. Was it to let me know that she had other options, we all do, and that art, like love, was a choice?

During my time with Yoshi she had arrived at my rooms one day, called by the landlord with concern. I had bought an air conditioner, with Yoshi's help. Workmen were cutting a hole in the wall to install it. I had not thought about Sensei as my guarantor, that she was responsible for me.

Now she was at the door. I led her into the main room, where my futon was still out. I sometimes was lazy and didn't put it away. A look of horror struck her and she tiptoed carefully around it, like evidence at a crime scene. That week, in a group lesson, she teased that she had walked in on me and Yoshi having sex.

"What? You did not!"

I didn't think about it as being anything other than her ruthless teasing. I wouldn't understand until much later how much the rumpled bedclothes had stimulated her imagination, and why.

I would not be able to leave Yoshi for some time. I stayed on for the worst reasons, from a sense of embarrassment. One bad choice meant staying on to defend it, and repair it, and I kept going, pained at the mistake but too proud to leave. To leave him would be to admit defeat.

9

... thawed for us in the palms of her hands ...

Sensei combed her repertoire for *oishii tokoro*, "tasty passages," to excerpt for her new show.

Whole songs were impossible. New students arrived by way of faxed maps on trains or scooters, with visa problems and teaching schedules, and had to be trained quickly. My role was to be a stable shamisen timekeeper, a holder of *ma*, space.

By late spring, she absorbed new students into the mix: Pres, an Australian flute player and vegetarian. At Gusto she now patted her tummy and said that she couldn't eat meat. Michael, a shaman studying matriarchal societies in Okinawa, would play hand bells and be Denise's stage hand. Sensei wanted to create, for the first time, a concert all her own, a note rung out from the center of her world.

She had enough students now, she said. We were improving. We didn't need the Japanese.

I spent more time practicing, often grabbing my shamisen as soon as I rolled out of the futon in the morning. A thick oiled print from my thumb now sat in the corner of my oak pick, no longer fresh and unmarked. I came home after work and continued, lighting long joss sticks that took forty-five minutes to burn, practicing until one burned out, sometimes lighting a second.

In late spring 1997, as the cherry blossoms began to open and viewing plans were made, a new song became the subject of much discussion, *Echigojishi*, "The Lion Dancers," composed in 1811 by Kineya Rokuzaemon X, the "Japanese Mozart." Sensei, as usual, made the song come alive. "The lion dancers come from the north," she said. "Way up, the snowy side, Niigata today. Used to be Echigo." Now there were mountains, ski slopes, and steaming hot spring pools surrounded by the cold white snowscape. "They come to the city to busk and make a money. Very lively, seducing young girls.… " She made an "O" with her mouth. "But they are homesick."

The images of the song were startling, placed next to each other for vividness and clarity: a bamboo cutter dreaming of flowers in bloom; a woman waiting under a pine tree on the beach for her lover, her passion as red as the maple leaves; the finely woven Ojiya cloth of the north.

Alan played the drums for *Echigojishi* in a Rising Sun headband, a muscle shirt, and googly glasses from a joke shop. He taught Sensei the word "jackass" and encouraged her to use it as he played, which she did, pronouncing it like some kind of Swedish greeting, "Ja-Khass!"

Alan was writing a play for this new show, an adaptation of an old noh play, *Kantan*, the only noh play written about a foreigner. In it, a Chinese pilgrim, Rosei, sets out to discover the meaning of life. He stops at a roadside inn to rest and is given a cypress pillow, on which he soon falls asleep. He is awakened by an imperial envoy declaring him emperor and is brought to a gilded palace, where he reigns for fifty years. When the innkeeper wakes him to tell him his rice is ready, Rosei realizes that his search is fruitless, that all life is an illusion, and goes home.

Alan's version featured a gaijin in Tokyo from Canton, Ohio, who fears that once he goes home his experience will have all been a dream. He was working on the play with three young Japanese actors who were eager to learn something about noh. Sensei's plan of returning to the Japanese their own discarded art forms was working. Kenneth, Sensei, Alan, and I were often together in those days. An intimacy developed over the music, an outing to kabuki, or a meal at Gusto, where we ordered steaks and pork cutlet sets and Sensei her usual mound of raw tuna over rice that always looked to me like a fresh wound. She would crane over it like a little bird, holding the hem of her hair away with her left hand as she brought the food to her lips. It was shocking how she could find something so horrid so delightful.

It was at Gusto that I learned that while I was in Kyoto with Yoshi, they'd chosen a concert venue.

"Yokohama," Sensei sighed. "So far...."

"It's not like it's Hokkaido," Alan said. "We'll drive you there in a rickshaw, OK?"

Sensei fake punched his arm. She named Kenneth musical director.

Sensei was more remote to me during those outings. Alan and Kenneth held doors for her, nicknamed her, brought gifts to her I would never consider—things she would never try on her own, unexpected things that I felt if I brought them would prompt her to say, Waste of time. My worst fear was that in this remark, she might mean me. They enlarged her in a way that I wanted to with music.

My playing was improving. Alan nicknamed me "Madame *Jozu*," meaning Skilled One. Denise had started calling me the star pupil. But the shamisen—I was learning the longer I played it—was hard. It was hard to play and even harder to perform. So much could go wrong. On your knees, legs prickling with pain, a sweaty palm on the pick. Strumming could get tangled, the notes curdle so easily sharp or flat.

Lessons were long, whole evenings or Sunday afternoons, with others or alone with Sensei, between meals and her laundry. While we played, she pruned my strokes but rarely gave an impression of how I was doing. I had only the mirror of her playing, across from me nightly, to see how I shored up. If I was not falling into the "live blanks," if my positions were dead on, and my notes dissolved with hers and our shamisen sounded like one, her voice darting and sailing overhead in its mismatched tilting thrall, that was success.

Sometimes I played with tapes from student recitals or professional concerts, but they were often too fast. *Renjishi* had many new techniques. The hard part was not learning each one, but ironing it out so that it flowed naturally through the piece, not calling attention to its difficulty. I couldn't do this with Sensei.

Our lessons were technically *okeiko*, literally "honoring the ancient teachings." This was your time with the master and it was not to be wasted. Once, at a lesson, when I was struggling with a difficult new passage, I stopped. "Hold on," I said. "Can we do that again?"

Sensei looked surprised but agreed. When I couldn't get it right the second time, I asked again. Again she agreed. But when I stopped a third time, she said, "Janet, that's what practice is for."

Okeiko was for taking in all you could from your teacher. You worked out the snags privately later.

I don't think I really knew how to practice back then. At the time, it meant to me doing the same thing over and over, and was boring. Mistakes were not interesting to me yet. Mistake still meant, "Wrong!" They were to be avoided and when they happened I often took a break, thinking maybe next time I'd miraculously get through it. I didn't see yet that a mistake was useful, that there was a way through it, that I could work something out on my own.

This was the lesson I needed most, but I had no words for how to ask for it, I had only the notes, the silences, the strings, and *kandokoro*, "intuitive places," on the shamisen neck. It's as if everything I wanted to say could only be said in the music.

I needed the lesson of the orange chest, I see now, of the mistress of the Gomokudo shop in Kyoto, and of my own abandoned piano lessons: the lesson on how to keep going—How does one endure? Like the music itself. Was it dying because people didn't care anymore? Or was it still alive? And what was the measure of that? As long as one person was playing it, was it still alive?

I went to Sensei's rooms more often. After lessons I helped her prepare a small meal, dried the dishes, put them away. One night, while she took her evening shower, I watched an NHK-TV special about traditional Japanese arts that she'd cued up for me with subtitles. A famous kabuki actor talked about the pose for Japanese dance being at the same center of gravity as when carrying an ice cube tray full of water to the freezer.

When she emerged from the bathroom in her miniature men's pajamas, her wet hair turbaned in a small towel, she asked, "Did you have nice viewing?"

Without her cape of hair, she was shorn of some power and her head looked enormous, like one of the doll heads at the puppet theater.

I told her about the ice cube tray theory.

She nodded. "Hmmm … useful."

I watched her begin to draw her hair dryer brush across her long dark strands. While I did so, I found myself hoping, that in one of those pulls across the brush, the neat arrangement of each patch at her neck until it was again her hair and no longer separated out, that she'd pull something out about me. Sitting there watching her until every last drop of the day was drained might give her time to reveal something about my studies. Perhaps she didn't want to say it in front of the other students. "You know, you're getting really good. Why don't we try a solo, just you and me? Are you ready for that?"

Instead, she spoke of Kenneth, "He is amazing." And Alan. "Kenneth is blue, you are red, but Alan is all colors. He is not human being."

Then she tucked away the dryer and the shark fin oil came out, and I knew that the evening was over. She walked me out and sat on the threshold between the kitchen and bath while I put on my shoes.

Life is ironic. We never know future.

If new knowledge about myself was iffy, there was always the larger picture, the universal perspective, and this soothed.

Walking home down the big road, it was dark, the streets filled with people coming home from work or evenings out with friends. The lights and sounds of Tokyo infused with the shamisen's bright sad twang, the kabuki actor's lecture about ice cubes, the hum of the hair dryer, and the scores in my backpack, my pick with its oiled thumbprint, bundled in a silk cloth.

"She is going to *okeiko*," Sensei would say with pride when seeing a picture of a maiko with a *furoshiki* cloth bundle in her arms on the streets. The apprentice had long sleeves, the *momo* peach hairstyle.

She was still a girl, not a woman yet, when she would become, finally, a geisha, a true "person of the arts."

≡

A few times, when leaving lessons Alan and I talked as he walked to the train station, or just sitting on the steps at Sensei's, blowing smoke rings at the moon. We wondered if Kenneth was good for Sensei? Would he leave? We feared a Madame Butterfly exit. But she could take care of herself. She had her own mission, I said.

What began as idle gossip with him had a great effect on me. Alan became a reference point for my experiences in Tokyo. He was good-looking, warm, approachable. He wore billowy linen shirts over muscle tees, long shorts, and sandals. He moved eagerly through Tokyo, and was passionate about Japan. When I first met him he had come from a festival where he had taken his VHS camera to film. Just looking at the big clunky camera made me embarrassed for him. But he didn't seem to mind sticking out as a foreigner.

Soon we started sliding into a booth at Gusto to order hamburger steaks and a Drink Bar, where we could get unlimited refills on hot or cold drinks. With Sensei, I would often return from my refill to find her at the cashier paying the tab so we could get home to practice. Once, she disappeared completely, and I found her halfway along the road to her rooms. Alan and I ate and drank and smoked right through to dessert—adzuki bean sundae for him, black tea cake for me—punctuating our talk of film, music, photography, Tokyo.

His metaphor for going home after living in Japan was virginity: you could never go back to holding hands. It changed you, he said at Gusto one night. "You can't go back. And yet you do. We all do. It's our nature. Like a salmon who swims upstream to mate and die. We can't help it."

He took a drag on his cigarette.

I knew Alan was thinking a lot about going home. He was a temporary visitor here to study the performing arts. He would go home in September to start graduate school.

But the image of the salmon and home confused me. "But what if leaving is better? Are you saying we're still drawn to go back home?"

"Basically, yeah. I just think it's a strong pull, something we've all got to reckon with."

The thought was electric. I couldn't say I agreed with it, but the fact that something tumbled out that made me *want* to think about it later—that I had to wrestle with—lit me up. My responses went this way and that, without regard to verb placement, word order, or anything that might confuse a non-native speaker. I was saying not what was expected of me, or what people wanted to hear, but trying to figure out my true feeling about something.

It made me homesick—for jokes, puns, double entendres, allusions to culture. A shared context—an alignment—had been missing. Talking to Alan, I remembered that I had majored in French, loved Camus and existential philosophy. He had opinions about everything, and so did I, I was realizing. Mostly we talked about Japan. Japan! It was a better way. We lamented our cities back home, the unsafe neighborhoods, the racism and hypocrisy. In Japan, there was dignity in all kinds of work, the valuing of people, communal sharing. You were never without a net or a purpose, there were people watching out for you, not like in America, competitive and isolated.

With Alan I confessed my embarrassments. I once bought miso paste thinking it was peanut butter. He said he once ate a block of hard *mochi* rice, not knowing it had to be cooked first. I bought sticky dessert rice by mistake and had a gooey mess at dinner! I didn't know which way to squat in Japanese toilets!

We crooned Steely Dan tunes, they were coming out of hiding for a tour! We talked about opera and Joseph Campbell. I brought him Nietzsche quotes from my journal. I could understand his humor: self-deprecating and absurd.

When he invited me to a kimono bargain sale with Philip, a friend from his gaijin house, I surprised myself by following them down the aisles, oohing and ahhing over the patterns and designs. I helped them choose souvenirs. They were both leaving Tokyo soon—it was always a revolving crew of expatriates, it seemed—and their nearness to departure let me be a foreigner again. With Alan I noticed anew the smell of bitter citron and soy in the air, the way the light hit the skyscrapers of Shinjuku.

We started meeting for long walks in Tokyo, taking off with a map and no plan. Alan could walk for hours on end. He didn't need to know where we were going. He trusted we'd end up somewhere, and we did: the perfume-scented halls of an arcade, a piss-strewn alley in Kabukicho, a window selling sweet potato ice cream.

I tired on these walks and wanted to turn back soon, but I followed him, determined to keep up with his long strides. There was so much to see, to photograph, to laugh at, even in the alleyways of Soapland, a red-light district with pictures of schoolgirls on sandwich boards outside strip joints, where men held signs that advertised, ANAL FUCK.

Yoshi often called when I was out with Alan. He had secured me a PHS cell phone on his family plan so we could talk anytime. Usually he called to ask me where I was. *"Ima doko?" "Chotto ... densha no naka ni ... "* "I'm on the train and can't talk." When I answered and was out with Alan, I cut the evening short. Back home, Yoshi would often be there—he was spending more time at my place—wanting to know where I was and with whom.

"You don't understand," I said. "We're just friends. Americans are like that. We don't separate out by genders like you do here."

"This is Japan, Roba-chan," Yoshi said.

At our lessons, Sensei would look out at the laundry drying on her balcony and marvel again at Alan's power. "Good person for you," she said. Like her compatible drum skins, we were "nice together."

I didn't need to convince Alan of anything or win him over. I didn't bump his elbow accidentally, bat my eyes, toss my hair. I didn't lure him into talking about his private life or assail him with pleas or phone calls. We tumbled out of Sensei's door and I could breathe again, slow down, think, in the cool night air.

There was no imbalance, no tilting out of reach, just our conversations, pausing, restarting, stopping again. I had found something important that I had yet to find in Tokyo: a friend. Not *deshi* or teacher, girlfriend or gaijin, or foreigner, the perpetual houseguest in the living room of Japan.

With Alan I was no one. I was me.

=

We passed into rainy season in early summer, 1997, and woke up one day to all the vending machines changed over from hot drinks to cold. Green tea, black tea, and Pocari Sweat, a cold, grapefruity "ion supply" drink for energy in the depleting Japanese summers.

One day, Alan and I were at Sensei's practicing. He kept asking if I was going to be a "lifer" and calling me Kurtz, the man gone round the twist in *Heart of Darkness*.

After a brief lunch and discussion of stage arrangements, I brought out pictures of me and Yoshi in Kyoto, in cotton robes in our room.

"Porno!" Sensei gasped.

"No it isn't!" I said, scooping them up.

"Just admit it, Janet," Alan teased.

"Jesus," I said later when we were sitting on a bench on the walking path to Shimokitazawa. "What would she do if she saw real porn?"

He laughed. We'd started stopping there with tall gold cans of Ebisu beer. It was starting to feel like we were manufacturing more ways to spend time.

"I think she thinks I'm a good influence on you."

"What do you mean?"

"To pull you back from Yoshi."

"Yeah," I said.

I had been suggesting Yoshi stay at his own house more often, claiming I had to practice for the concert. But the more I distanced myself from him, the more he pursued me. I didn't know how to leave. When my cell phone rang. I stuffed it deeper into my bag.

"You don't have to live like that," Alan said.

"Ha. Look who's talking." Alan had told me of his cheating girl-friend back home.

The next time out in Tokyo we couldn't make out the name of a department store in the crease of my Tokyo atlas. It looked like My Load. It was My Lord. This became a running shorthand for us, one that could send us screeching with laughter. Loads were the burdens we carried willingly, no matter how bad for us. We started toasting to life without contortions. No loads! I shut down my phone. He broke up with Claire. We crooned the lyrics to "Dr. Wu" under a full moon.

=

There was a drama at Sensei's, *always*. It never left, like her hair, a severe curtain of cuts and lines to be viewed from different angles. She could chew on details incessantly, especially a slight or indignity. "I am human being," she would say. As we planned for her unique show, in which we'd perform without professional Japanese back-up, her hapless victimhood increased and I didn't understand where it came from. She would take excessive amounts of time from a lesson or meal to justify herself in the face of some intrusion on her pride—a coworker, a fellow Japanese musician, her teacher's wife. They could all set her darkly aboil, the barb bobbing to the surface of a lesson or meal for days, with no seeming development of insight or psychology. Just a pressurized familiar release of the same echo—"I am human being"—until finally she would say to me, "Anyway, Janet"—as if it were I who was holding onto the grudge—"we have many things to do, we shouldn't distract" and I'd never hear about it again. Like a thorn plucked from a thumb, the wound healed.

Alan and I talked about it all the time on our walks. I had taken to showing him some of my favorite haunts in Shinjuku: jazz CD shops, a Thai buffet, places to buy funky eyeglasses, the best pens.

Alan said Sensei called him sometimes on the hall phone at the gaijin house late at night.

I kept walking, embarrassed for some reason. "Really? What does she say?"

"Well, she's vague. She says she's worried about Kenneth but doesn't say why."

"What does she mean, worried?"

He shook his head. "Mainly I just try to make her laugh. She can get so damn dark."

Alan and Sensei both brought large numbers of people together for a sole purpose—music and theater, temporary and intense—and when it was over, it was like his question about Japan: which was more real, the stage, or the life you went back to? "Everything I care about is invisible," Sensei once told me.

One evening I took Alan to Sangenjaya, an old neighborhood walkable from Sensei's. Tokyo had so many of these jewels on its backstreets. The glass towers and video screens were only downtown. These other areas were quiet, local, with women batting futons in the sun on a Saturday morning, and small shops hawking their wares. Sangenjaya was known for tea. Its vending machines carried Gyokuro, Jewel Tea, the finest of Kyoto. It also had a 1940s movie theater, and, as you could tell from all the smokestacks poking up like steeples in a New England town, numerous *sento*, public baths.

Sensei hated *sento*. She had grown up without a bath or hot water, having to walk in robe and slippers with her toiletries down the road to the neighborhood baths. To me the baths were an almost spiritual rite. The soak was intense, up to 105 degrees, so hot you had to hold cold water in your mouth, or a cold towel on your head. I never had trouble taking off my clothes and washing among the Japanese, probably because I was a foreigner, so different that what could it matter?

My favorite was a 1930s bathhouse that I had found by accident, noticing the wood pile out back and the dark blue split curtain with the kanji for *yu*, hot water. The Mama-san was a crinkled old woman who took your ¥500 coin and returned to her soap opera with a smile. She sat on a raised platform between the men's and women's baths to keep an eye on both sides.

Alan loved baths as much as I did. We waved at each other that night and entered our separate bathing areas. I could hear men's voices echoing on the tiles over the divider. Alan always took longer, and that night I was sitting outside sipping a beer when he staggered out, a towel around his neck, pink-cheeked and woozy.

We were headed for an interesting-looking beer garden, when Sensei called me.

"Hi Janet, where are you?"

She asked if we had eaten and wanted to come for dinner and more rehearsing.

Alan and I looked at each other. "We can be there in about twenty minutes," I said. There was never any question that we'd go. More than once, headed out on an adventure, we would be drawn back to her dusky rooms, where she had treats waiting: tasty fish, pork-stuffed buns, and glutinous rice wrapped in a salted cherry leaf that she had frozen and now thawed for us in the palms of her hands.

=

If I was the star of the show, as Denise said, I didn't feel like it. One afternoon at a lesson, Alan and Kenneth suggested Sensei and I play a duet from *Renjishi*.

"What?" she asked. "Why?"

Sensei's reply was crushing though I knew it was just her English. She needed time to train newcomers. She needed energy for Kenneth. Jealousy felt small.

She was reluctant, but after much teasing, she agreed it was a beautiful piece and that she and I should play it together. I was elated. After that, I didn't mind fetching tea for Kenneth or serving snacks to Alan. At home, I settled onto my practice cushion, lit a joss stick, and didn't stop until I got the fast slippery sprints of *Renjishi* under my fingers. I parsed out the *ma*, spaces, until I could predict them with ease, incorporating the silences into the long lines of sound.

I also in those last weeks before the show, despite Sensei's insistence, had a kimono made to order, a summer *ro* weave, the material of the kimono she was wearing when I met her the year before. I asked Yoshi to come with me to a kimono seller in Shinjuku to negotiate the robe.

"Kimono not important," Sensei said. "Don't waste your money."

She recommended ready-to-wear washable robes off the rack

that she bought at Midori-ya in the old town, Asakusa, in XL "monster size," she said, to accommodate hips and height.

The robe I bought was sheer and light. The sleeves fell right to where they were supposed to: stopping at the bones of the wrist. The obi was sheer silk, too, in a very pale green. The silk scarf to hold the obi was a fresh mint. The robe itself had a white pattern of cherry blossoms on the skirt and sleeves. Everything fit me, finally. The color I chose was salmon.

=

They say musicians have more in common with each other than people in their own culture. With Sensei, I remembered things I had forgotten: days spent at the piano working on something, a sense of purpose that had been lacking since I quit, afraid that I could never be good enough.

She was right. Music had no border. In it, you were all part of a blissful oceanic joy. It was the return that was painful, the remembering you were ultimately alone.

Did culture have a border? If not, then what was it? Where did it reside? Alan's play, *Canton*, was a way to talk about his own fears of leaving Japan and the whole experience vanishing as if it were a dream. And in a way, mustn't it? How did one take home such a thing? What to do with it? Was Japanese music cultural taxidermy, a remnant you could hear, a window into the past? What did it mean to be alive?

These were the things I was thinking about as we headed into the performance that August. There were no answers, only more questions.

I wanted to ask Sensei how to leave Yoshi. He'd started sending me letters on handmade paper, or calligraphy on small flat coasters. *I love you! Marry me!* Mementos from dates arrived in plain brown envelopes, as if the sight of chopstick wrappers, bar coasters, and amusement park ticket stubs would change my mind. *Come back! I don't want to make you one of my memories!* "Before I was just dancing," he said, pleading for another chance. His words became more cryptic. *I am facing west. It feels like snow.* He threated to chug Drano, calling and saying, "That's it, goodbye!" gurgling off the line.

During our final rehearsals of the duet—of lions dancing with butterflies—I started crying. "It's too hard. I can't do it."

Sensei was alarmed "Are you okay?" she said, squinting, as if into a too-bright light.

I told her I wasn't feeling well. I had a stomachache. She brought me medicine—nasty black pellets she said were used at the Russian front—and told me to get some rest.

I left feeling like I had ruined something pure with my tears. Tears were too natural, too real, and in this they were frightening. When Sensei talked to her daughters she was familiar but not affectionate. *"Eh, Naochan, oyasumi,"* she said on the phone in the evenings, more a string of ritual syllables than a conversation. But the point was keeping deep feelings hidden. Surfacing meant almost to dilute them, and how could it be real if it was given so cheaply? Only what was valued stayed invisible.

Tears were out of place because they didn't recognize the border between the two worlds, the world you kept for yourself and the world you showed to others.

It's as if by showing my tears, I was showing a loss of control that must have felt frightening to her.

=

The morning of *Canton*, August 9, 1997, was unusually clear and windy, a day more like the post-typhoon calm of October than late summer. In the early hours there had been an earthquake, a sudden rupturing as if to remind us of the atomic blast on Nagasaki fifty-two years earlier.

We arrived at the Yokohama Noh Theater in the morning laden with instruments, scores, kimono, foods, and programs. It took hours just to organize and dress. The smooth wooden stage was bare but for a backdrop of a lone pine tree painted in feathery green strokes.

One of Sensei's coworkers had set up an easel at the side of the stage to post song titles in elegant calligraphy. Mrs. Yamaguchi, Sensei's rich friend who had furnished my rooms with designer cast-offs, was there with rice crackers and tea for snacks. We rolled two strips of red felt carpeting in a ninety-degree angle on the stage to protect our knees from the floor.

"So gorgeous," Sensei said as each gaijin emerged in kimono, especially the men in *hakama*, a formal split-skirt that made them look regal and commanding.

"Look!" Kenneth said, pointing out NHK-TV setting up a boom mic at the stage's edge. He and Sensei went to introduce themselves to the reporters. We were excited. There was always a chance the Japanese might notice Sensei and appreciate her efforts. A news camera was promising.

We played two sold-out shows to audiences mixed with foreign and Japanese, young and old, both sitting as still for the music as for the drama. An older gentleman was in tears at *Kojo no Tsuki,* "Moonlight Over Ruined Castle," a folk song popular after Japan's defeat, when the country learned that the emperor was not a divine being descended from the Sun Goddess, but a fallible human being speaking over the radio.

In *Canton,* I made two nearly fatal errors: I had gone onstage without my *yubikake,* knit finger sling, forcing my left hand to skid and leap around the neck rather than slide smoothly. Then, after sitting on my knees for twenty minutes, I nearly toppled over as I stood up. I grabbed Kenneth's shoulder and almost took him down with me.

Yoshi had been there, I knew from the flashbulbs in my eyes. He called when I was in the parking garage smoking with Alan afterward.

You were so good," he said

"I'm going out."

"I know."

Another candle party: *Look what we did, gaijin loosed on the world! Another heist!* Sensei beamed as she stepped over the piled coats and legs to set the table with radish salad, fried chicken, sushi, and beer. Pres brought a bottle of Australian port that was to replace her plum spritzer from now on. Sensei raised a glass of it to her lips. Pink shot into her cheeks. "My seduction," she said.

"Shameless hussy!" Alan roared.

She did her geisha move: a cuddle of the neck, and then opened her mouth in an "O."

Kenneth turned on the evening news and found a thirty-second blurb about gaijin playing traditional Japanese music. The camera scanned the audience, stopping to focus on Kenneth and me. I was glad they didn't catch me nearly falling on my numb ankles. The clip made no mention of Sensei.

Pres was outraged. "Aw, blimey! Look what she's doing, man!"

As we chided the reporter, Sensei lay her head lazily on a bamboo pillow next to Alan's knees. "Alan-chan, you can't leave Japan. We can make another concert." She tugged his sleeve.

How could she not expect anything? I envied her ability to be unattached to the outcome of her shows, and I envied even more how she would suffer this again and she seemed to know this and would keep on doing it. She would stay up all night, washing, cleaning, rinsing herself of the day. *It's over,* she said after a show. She could let it go and be empty.

Her capacity for endings was breathtaking. This was her art, these beheadings that made me stand back and touch all my limbs. *Tomorrow is new life.* She would start again, building another repertoire to play, training new hands on the shamisen's neck. She had, you see, mastered loss.

I had not. Looking back, I see that this time was one of great happiness and alignments. For a moment, everyone's differences—the chafing and bumping up against each other—disappeared. The shamisen became something new, something it had never been before. But it still touched all the places in me I knew well. It remained unreachable, unrequitable, unattainable. I see only now that this is the point.

≡

This part of the story is the moment of the widest opening, the deepest learning. Like a camera shutter opening to swallow all the happy faces. Where did they all scatter to? How did they end up? It is the acme of Sensei's work and mine together. In the pictures from the performance she stands in the front row, holding a noh mask, raising it up from its pink silk pillow in the cypress box, its olive ribbon undrawn. She would never be so beautiful to me, so glamorous, so clearly and truly my teacher. Who can forget that cape of hair, the red in the corners of her eyes? And the thing I rarely saw and never would again: I saw her top teeth. Usually hooded by her painted pink lips, hidden even when wisecracking in her kitchen, it defied all Japaneseness. She had truly achieved something, I think, though she would never speak of it. I thought we had just begun, but looking back now, I see we had gotten to the end of a road.

I would leave Sensei at the door that night and go to a party to fill up on laughter, music, wine. To listen to Chet Baker croon, "It had to be you," and drink Okinawan wine with a fat snake in the bottom of the heavy glass, a gift from Michael, the shaman, who gave us Japanese sparklers, branches of twisted paper that, when held upside down, released a soft purr of snowflakes.

And when Alan pulled me onto his lap, I would hold on to his collar and hang on, my breath catching on his as we kissed, the cicadas sizzling above, the air like soup around my legs and arms, the heat unbearable, unstoppable, our hands, our lips.

The only way forward now was back.

≡

And I knew by now something about yearning.

As Alan had been saying during *Canton*, you are always where you came from, no matter how far you travel. It was our instinct, our humanness. Mastery, one could say, is becoming what you are, not what you aren't. But back then I believed that I could escape the past and start again by becoming someone new, changing the surface, taking on a new role.

All this applied to Sensei, too, which I did not see at the time. The more I heard, the more blind I became, as if one sense eroded the other. She, too, was a product of where she came from. We couldn't exist floating in the kitchen around a candle flame forever. We were who we were. It was bound to catch up with us sometime. Like the music and its future, how much could you change? What was it wise to change, and what not? All these things I didn't ask until much later, when it was too late.

The kiss with Alan led to a talk the next day. We'd ended up at a Royal Host on the big road past Sensei's, kissing and talking all night. Walking there from the party we passed my apartment, which Alan had visited before with Sensei and Kenneth, which is to say, he knew it was there, that we were passing it, as I knew. Had neither of us thought of going there? It must have crossed my mind. I was usually quick to quench a lit fire, excitable, impulsive. I wonder now if it felt too close to Sensei, not morally wrong, but situationally wrong. Had duty set in so deeply that we sat now in self-denial on the bench under the cherry trees again, en route to Sensei's house, as usual, to watch the post-concert video, share a meal, play music?

This is what it was. We two were no longer we two. That's why we didn't go to my apartment. Because even there, just the two of us, we wouldn't be alone.

=

On the bench, we talked about the kiss. We held hands maybe. I remember warmth, friendship, his presence nourishing me, even in my frustration at his leaving, at the unfairness.

"But how will you ever know what this could lead to? Are you going to just give all this up? What a crock!"

The kiss was just that. He couldn't stay. He had to get back. He'd moved before to be with someone—he always did, it seemed, and it never worked.

I've done that my whole life, I thought. Isn't that what you did for love?

≡

Things get fuzzy here—or did at the time. I think now I could probably sort it out. But back then it was like Sensei when she asked me at lessons to play "less sticky." I would ask what she meant and she would answer only by showing me her own pick flying cleanly over the strings. She couldn't explain how to get there.

Everything around the music was sticky, the connected orbits, the mental murkiness that Alan had been pulling me out of so that I could see my own shape again, think my own thoughts. But at the time it was hard to see motives, responsibility. I remember only scenes, fragments, rising up now in the music of my own memory.

The group went to Kyoto sightseeing two days after the concert. This time, to avoid *soraori*, the return of drear ordinary life, Sensei had people join her on her escapade. Kenneth, Alan, Jane, and Brian went. I had to teach and stayed behind in the oppressive Tokyo heat. At night, Alan called from the road. I snuck out of the futon if Yoshi was there to talk to him in the kitchen.

"I'm pining for you," he said.

"Me, too," I said, and listened to his stories about Sensei and the group.

I sensed Yoshi was awake when I got back into the futon, but I didn't care. Within a few days, I asked for my key back. He dropped it into a box of condoms that he sealed with adhesive tape, and handed it to me as he walked out.

I remember sitting in Sensei's rooms with her and Denise, in the air conditioned cool, after Sensei came back from Kyoto. Denise was readying for her return to China. They told me it might be a good idea to leave Tokyo for a while. If Yoshi did something foolish I could be deported.

I knew Alan was headed for the Inland Sea, a narrow body of water that separated the main island of Japan from hundreds of tiny islands, some no bigger than a lone twisted pine. He wanted to write a play about it. Our only plan was to have pancakes again when he returned to Tokyo, before he headed back to the States.

Go to him, they seemed to be saying, or I was hearing. I remember the relief at someone uttering my own thoughts because those thoughts felt unreachable, taboo, even. It jibed with something I remembered from a dinner at Gusto with Alan. We were eating hamburgers and slurping iced coffees, talking greedily, deeply, windingly getting lost and not concerned about finding our way out. One time his voice receded, and I found myself floating away for a minute, and a small voice inside rising up inside me that said, "Run away with me. Let's get out of this place together."

$$=$$

We stayed away for ten days.

The waters of the Inland Sea were calm and protected. These are ancient lands, the oldest in Japan some say. There is where the Genji battles raged, and where the Heike fell. By the time Alan and I were sailing its harbors, a bridge had been built to the mainland of Honshu, and modern life was encroaching.

Matsuyama. Konpira. Takamatsu.

We visited old kabuki theaters and shrines, and sat up all night talking on a sea wall outside a sesame oil factory, the air smoky and sweet. We ate noodles in mild broth, and talked to Okinawans who were pilots in the war.

On Miyajima, deer loped in and out of the ferry station, poking their velvety noses into our pockets for sweets. Children, followed by grandparents in cotton summer robes from the island's hot spring hotel, squealed at their long tongues lapping their chubby fingers. We sat on a rock and gazed at Itsukushima Shrine, one of the most famous views in Japan, just as the sun was setting behind its red *torii* gate, standing tall like a giant bird's perch in the mud beds at low tide. For the first time we didn't talk about Japan. It was as if the referents we revisited each time we'd met in Tokyo to talk and explore were no longer needed. The sun dissolved, the twilight deepened, and a row of stone lanterns along the shoreline lit up like a gold watchband.

I had not seen the countryside of Japan, only its throbbing cities. Life was slower, friendlier. No one pointed or tried to speak English with us or thought of us at all, it seemed. We ate dinner at the only restaurant on the island, a small spot that sold Hiroshima-style *okonomiyaki*, pancakes stuffed with noodles and garlic, run by a Mama-san and her sixteen-year-old daughter. Alan plied her with questions in English and she lingered, giggling, as her mother brought us plates of the pancakes and pickles.

As soon as I'd arrived and met up with Alan at the Tourist Information Center at Hiroshima Station, I didn't know what to say or do. Why had I come? He hadn't asked me to.

From the train, I had seen the Genbaku Dome, the top of the last building standing in the center of the atomic blast, now looking like a crown of thorns scraping the sky. There was so much to remember in Japan, and, in many ways, this trip would be a long forgetting. We carried our bags down the hot dusty streets by the sea, and finally, into Philip's apartment where Alan was staying, a high rise with a balcony overlooking the city.

It was during the eating of that pancake on Miyajima that I floated off again, as I had at Gusto, and felt the reality that we weren't in Tokyo anymore. That we'd peeled apart and would forever be changed. Perhaps this is what love is: a readiness more than a desire. It was like my first day at Sensei's when I'd slipped my toe in that tabi and said, "Yes, I'll do it."

We thought no further of the return to Tokyo, but hung, bobbing on boats in the waters, letting the sea buoy our denial of where we'd come from and would arrive at eventually. There was only the next port, the next ship's deck, and the soft curves of the Aegean-like waters and its spooky ports, arriving with no more than a map and our bags and a desire to explore each other. No news reached us from Tokyo, not even of the death of Princess Di, in a car crash in a tunnel in Paris.

We slept on decks of ships and woke up, salted and sea-sprayed. We took pictures of our faces, cheeks red, eyes wild, besotted witnesses. We went from hot spring to hot spring, scrubbing our skin with salt then rinsing it all off in the baths. There was no unfulfilled keening, no brittle snap of the shamisen string. Groggy and logy, dozing in denial, we swam in the soft green-blue sea and sank in its gentle swells.

"Why not stay here?" we asked ourselves at a new grotto or beach, a tiny town with a shrine and a noodle shop. We knew we would not, but it felt important to wonder out loud, to take possession of ourselves in this new way. It was the magical thinking of the newly in love, who believe they can conquer anything. And it was an error in judgment, for the benevolent universe that had generously bestowed its hand on us was also the universe we knew, with its one person, like a tiny sun, at its center.

=

"Tadaima!"

Kenneth answered Sensei's door and let us in. *"Okaeri,"* she called from her stool in the music room. When we came around the corner she was gesturing to Kenneth to continue the music. Alan and I retreated to the kitchen until they finished.

It was Alan's last night in Japan. We'd been back only a couple of days, and he wanted to come say goodbye to Sensei. We'd been trying to find out all we could about each other before he left. We took long baths and stayed up late talking in the futon, often falling asleep midsentence. We went through our souvenirs, held each other, and one night, after I played an open mic with Kenneth and Judy, in which my shamisen went horribly out of tune, we came home and danced to "Black Cow." I was nervous about coming to see Sensei as a couple.

When Sensei and Kenneth emerged from their music, I poured us all glasses of cold barley tea.

"I'm teaching Kenneth new piece," Sensei said, sipping. "Tricky, but he is so good."

She made no mention of the Inland Sea, though we'd written and called her with our news.

"So how was the trip?" Kenneth asked.

"You can't leave Japan," Sensei pouted, tugging at Alan's sleeve. "You're my lover, too."

Alan teased her about her seductions.

Sensei announced Kenneth's singing debut the following summer at her teacher's *benkyo-kai*, a special recital where he'd be evaluated on the spot, like the Queen's students after the museum concert.

We played *Echigojishi*, and I finally felt like we were on the same page. But the festival-like mood of the music sounded halting and strained, Sensei's voice jagged and bleak. When Alan exaggerated his drum calls as usual, she asked him to be less expressive. She corrected my playing numerous times, and when I stopped to ask what my error was she shook her head. "Don't worry."

I made an attempt to bring her into our coupling. "We'd never have met without the shamisen or you," I said.

"Life is unexpected," was all she said.

Kenneth asked questions while Sensei stood quietly peeling fruit. We shared our adventure in the old kabuki theater, where we were allowed to peek into trap doors for trick entrances. I told Sensei we had found the Shimabara, an old pleasure quarter in Kyoto. The neighborhood was empty except for its huge gate and willow tree, and rows of old wooden houses, dark behind slatted doors. Alan and I had remarked on the ghostly spirits lingering there. Sensei nodded. She had seen it before.

I stared into my teacup. Her lifeless comments, her feigned ignorance, her flirtation with Alan, all stung like the violent snap of a shamisen string. Sitting in her rooms with the air conditioning on so low I was still sweating, the tea not chilled enough to quench my thirst, her rooms felt dark and shadowy, her hair a scary cloak, a witch's cape. A hot dryness rose in my throat.

In that moment, I hated her.

=

Sadness is prized in Japan. On the shamisen it is tended and constructed in the slow painstaking lines of sound, in notes that required morbid exacting, like the careful nightly arranging of Sensei's hair. In music one could find not hot tears but a cool comfortless human sadness that was bigger than you. Tears were too personal, too dissolving of form. They were a burden on others. Sadness held aloft could be metabolized into song. This is one of the most useful lessons I learned with Sensei, that one could find a use for melancholy.

After Alan left, in my apartment on the faded mats, the suitcases from the Inland Sea spilled out, as if retching onto the floor: hand towels, incense, soap, beads, a long Japanese pipe, sake cups, charms and chimes and everywhere the smell of sulfur and salt. The sight of the objects was too loaded with feelings. The only respite was to assemble, piece by piece, a shrine. It was a very Japanese thing to do. I stored everything in an antique sewing box and put it in the *tokonoma* alcove. Above it I hung the creased map from our journey, tracing with a yellow highlighter our route down the spine of Japan: from Tokyo to Hiroshima, to Miyajima, to Shikoku, to Shodoshima, to Osaka, to Tokyo.

Sensei reminded me that I needed my own life, and I nodded, letting her dote on me, inviting me for meals and to her practice sessions with Kenneth. She encouraged me not to think too much about Alan and gave me a new challenge—a capo, the very same that I'd found in the bottom drawer of my shamisen stand. A capo was a tiny sliver of wood that tightened around the shamisen's strings. A capo offered texture and variety, raising the tones one octave into a celestial plinking free of the main melody. One secured the capo with a *koyori*, a twisted strand of paper that slipped under the strings. Sensei had a drawer of several she had bought from the only maker in Tokyo. He had recently died, she said, in that way she had of delivering dire news in a matter of fact way. I think it helped her accept it. She often told me, "Janet *shoganai*, it can't be helped," when I protested an unfair ritual, a thieving student.

I accepted the fragile band of paper, felt its lightness in my hands, and the loss of the craftsman mixed with thoughts of the sunlit waterways of the Inland Sea, the copper light on Alan's skin. Everything rolled into one heaving sadness, like the paper itself, twisted tightly until all the individual folds had disappeared.

PART III

10

... it took an act of violence to be born ...

Once, at a lesson, I noticed in horror that the protective half-moon of paper on the shamisen sound box was unpeeling under my pick. I had been strumming at an incorrect angle and now I'd ruined the instrument. Sensei told me not to worry. I followed her into the kitchen, where she cracked an egg white into a teacup, dipped her ring finger in, and smoothed the goopy liquid along the paper, adhering it once again to the skin.

"There," she said, rinsing her finger. "Should work." She put on the kettle for tea.

The familiar tick-tick of the blue flame catching soothed. How much Sensei had taught me started to frighten me. It was like a very heavy weight, one I wanted to get free of but also be consumed by. I wanted to give everything. But no matter how much I gave, I would never know enough. I could never catch up. For every new thing I learned there were ten thousand things I would not.

I filed away the egg white trick but didn't record it anywhere, like my Sicilian grandmother's recipes. After she died, they realized she'd written none of it down. The thick white pizzas, the anisette cookies. Why would she? She was there.

Most dangerously, my worries blinded me to the possibility of what we all might mean to Sensei. I had not yet started to consider that she might need us, too.

=

Of all the changes Japan has been through, it has never, like many of its Asian sisters, been a colony. Instead, it has taken what it needed of the cultures who entered it and made something new with it of its own. Learn the thing trying to defeat you and you cannot lose. This is truly creative, for nothing is made that has not existed before in some way. It is also, I have come to see, an act of resistance. Fusing with the colonizer you may lose a part of yourself but you will still be alive. It is a refusal to die.

The shamisen itself is an expansion of the Chinese *san sien*, "three string," which landed in Okinawa in 1603. When it arrived on the mainland, blind players of the *biwa* lute took to it and started to change it. They covered the head with the skin of dog or cat instead of snake. They lengthened the neck, increased the size of the sound-box. The pick, too, changed from a sliver of bamboo to the larger wooden plectrum, weighted to move like a lever over the strings.

But over time, change in the music was not allowed. If one wanted to, for example, change the *ma*, spaces, in a piece, or use a different drum pattern, one had to start a whole new school. The penalty for innovation was exile. There could only be one way, *ryu*, one school, one teacher to belong to. They were like bloodlines. You only had one family.

In the same way, you belonged to one teacher. Sensei spoke often of her teacher of thirty-five years in terms of her belonging to him. If you left a teacher, you gave them a sort of reverse dowry, paying a large sum for all the income they would lose in your wake.

At first it seemed unrealistic that students would not grow and gravitate to new teachers. They might need new things the old teacher couldn't give. But in my next period of time with Sensei—I had not been there that long, just over a year, and yet it felt like several—it became very clear to me why having two teachers was not preferable. It was, in fact, impossible.

=

After Alan left Japan, two things kept me busy: learning the capo to help Kenneth practice for his *benkyo-kai* and studying the drums, neither by choice but by necessity. Drums would be useful for Sensei's concerts, and so that fall, she brought us to her teacher for lessons. Because it was Sensei's own teacher, and she was, in effect, "sharing" us with her, it was not breaking any rules. The extra income for a female musician, who didn't get as many gigs as men, didn't hurt, either.

Drum lessons were in Musashi-Koyama, a neighborhood in Meguro, a few stops away on the Yamanote Line or two bus connections. Sensei always preferred the bus. I arrived at her house at 7 a.m. to help carry her bags. Kenneth and Jane would already be at the bus stop, swapping Friday night stories. Had we heard of the new restaurant in Roppongi designed like Alcatraz where you ate in a simulated prison cell?

We always arrived first at the *keikoba*, training space, which was a noh stage in a high-rise apartment that belonged to a friend of Kikuyu-sensei, Sensei's and now our drum teacher. The friend's husband was an amateur noh actor. Many people studied traditional arts for the discipline and for the atmosphere of elegance. The stage was smooth and pale and quiet as we traveled it in our socks, fetching red carpets and floor cushions, depositing one in front of the lone painted pine for our teacher. There was a hush beyond just the early hour. It was as if setting up for the entrance of royalty. A noh actor once told me that if he could choose one word to describe Japan it would be "respect." At the core was not religion but reverence. It was awe I was feeling, of ancestral forms passed down in the bodies of ordinary people, elevating them to worshipful heights.

Kikuyu-sensei looked like any other *obaasan*, elder lady, on the train, her coif dyed with a slight blue tinge, with age spots on her cheeks and hands, and a raspy voice from her many years of smoking. She had grown up in a temple in Kamakura, the daughter of a Buddhist priest. She had been a dancer for a long time, which accounted for the girlish, almost kittenish, tilt of her head as she played the *taiko*, a small stick drum, for which she was known to be the best in all Japan. She played the low-strung drum in front of her, rising slightly on her legs and cocking an ear, as if listening to a conversation. She struck the drum easily but with force. I never thought she was going to make it in time. Her strikes seemed almost lazy, drumsticks raised up above her head in balletic poses, chin tucked girlishly, and I'd think anxiously, Now! Go! and she'd bring the stick down perfectly, not a moment too soon or too late.

Sensei nodded. "Many players are early, they are too eager."

When we heard her car pull into the garage, Kenneth, Jane, and I went down in the elevators to grab the drums from the trunk of her white Toyota. Upstairs, she settled onto a cushion at the head of a long table and lit a cigarette. She greeted Sensei using *"-chan,"* the diminutive. She had known Sensei since she was sixteen. She was like a benevolent and fearsome aunt that we all loved. We bowed low to her on our knees, slipped her envelopes of money. We assembled each of her *taiko*, cradling the drum head on its stand and sliding the two drumsticks underneath at a thirty-degree angle.

Other students arrived. Kikuyu-sensei crushed out her cigarette and brought her tall wooden box to the front of the room. From a zippered pouch she removed two long leather fans.

And our lesson would begin.

=

When we started studying drums it was as if a child hovering in the corner was now brought to the center of the room. I had seen Sensei interact with her drums for some time. Their tan polished faces peeked out from her bookshelves during shamisen lessons. There were her drum-collecting trips to Kyoto, her drum lessons penciled in on the gas calendar in Japanese. Sometimes she sat at the kitchen table as we snacked, holding a *tsuzumi* drum on her shoulder as if burping a small baby. Then, bringing it down onto her lap, she tuned it by adjusting its long orange hemp ropes and affixing a piece of *washi* paper to the rear skin with her middle finger, moistened with water from a nearby tiny cup. Then she brought the skin to within an inch of her lips and breathed on it in husky respirations, moving the drum to cover all of the skin with her long damp breaths. Unlike shamisen, whose wood swelled in humidity, causing the skins to split, drums loved moisture.

At the time I was carrying around a small Dover notebook with a cover of Edvard Munch's *The Scream* to write down unusual words Sensei used. *Soraori*, "the sky falling" after a performance; *ochitsuki no basho*,"cozy place"; *me o koyasu*, "tired eyes after browsing all day at antiques"; and the word she used most often to refer to drums: *zeitaku*, which she translated as "so gorgeous."

Zeitaku meant lavishness when one could hardly afford it, like spending your last ¥5,000 on a taxi ride. Deprivation and denial could be turned on their heads—a kind of decadent jujitsu—and, with a flick of the wrist, rendered replete, desirable. The other word the noh actor used to describe Japan was "scarcity culture." The U.S. was "plus culture," Japan was "minus culture."

Zeitaku was an expense you couldn't *not* afford. It was luxury but not monetary. It was the richness of experience, even if it put you in debt, especially so. Sensei's life in music was *zeitaku*. Her concerts, like *Canton*, often ran her into the red several thousand dollars. I was always aghast when I heard these figures and thought, "Well, that's the end of that. How could it continue?" But it did, however harrowing.

Nothing was more *zeitaku* than the *tsuzumi*: two hides of unborn horse (a lavish sacrifice, she agreed) lashed with tangerine hemp ropes, the stitching on its tender skin dotted with petals of black lacquer. When a skin tore—some were a hundred years old or more—it was brought to the one man in Tokyo who could repair them and stayed with him for up to six months. When it came back, the cracks were not sealed and invisible. There was no attempt at all, in fact, to hide the imperfection. The broken places were filled with gold, threading their way across the surface like precious new veins to be tapped.

This fragility was part of its power, I think, to transform in a way the shamisen did not. I feared when Sensei let her students play her priceless drums, but she ran to get her camera. With a *tsuzumi* in their hands, the student was no longer an ordinary being, but brought to some rarefied place of beauty.

Learning drums was supposed to make us better shamisen players. Japanese musicians were expected to study a second or third form just for themselves, It would never be performed on stage. It was a training in empathy, the fine art of attunement. But I worried that drums would dilute my playing and take away time I could be spending memorizing pieces. Because I could not afford a drum of my own, it meant more time at Sensei's with Kenneth and Jane and others, learning together.

I couldn't say no, even if I wanted to. Saying no wasn't allowed, even though, as a foreigner, the rules didn't apply. I felt I had already said yes by everything that had come before. By taking on the shamisen, by slipping on that tabi, I had committed to it all. I had agreed to be led. I couldn't jump out in this one area. I couldn't cherry-pick my musical preferences.

I had tried once, after hearing a new piece at a recital called *Ume no Sakae,* a ballad about plum blossoms written for a girl's wedding.

"Just technique, Janet. No feeling," Sensei said when I inquired casually about learning it. What she meant was that *Ume no Sakae* had no cranes or magical foxes making swords. It was unhinged from the legends of Edo. No story. No seduction.

To me, "Plum Ballad" was like her collection of ivory picks. One evening before a concert, I had arrived to check in and found her circling the music table, gazing down at a half dozen of them. It was the same shape and size as the pick I used, of flecked oak, but these were of varying shades of white, creamy, and opaque.

"What are you doing?" I asked.

"Which one to use tomorrow for stage," she said, weighing one in her palm.

"Where did you get them?"

"Some sensei gave to me."

"Where can you get one?" I asked.

She waved her hand. "Don't waste your money, Janet."

Obtaining an ivory pick became an obsession, and each time

I mentioned it, she said the same thing. "Don't waste your money." Then one day she handed me a tan rectangular box. I opened it eagerly and found inside a new pick of flecked oak. The smooth untouched wood with its sharp angled edges and a slip of washi paper around the weighted handle with the tiny initials of the maker was the ugliest object I'd ever seen. I despised even more my desire for something she could not afford to give.

"Plum Ballad," I suggested, would be a good performance piece. Finally I arrived to find a copy of the score at my place at the music table, covered with a picture of an old woodblock of a woman under plum blossoms in snow, her flat garish features almost horror-strewn.

The song was laced with tricks. There were four solos with fast pizzicatos that required control and speed in the strumming hand. One swirled around the note 4# to imitate a snowstorm.

Snow is the hardest thing to depict on the shamisen. It was either the low, slowly accumulating tattoo of a gentle snowfall, or the fast buzzing whirl of a squall, requiring a deep pressing technique that could easily trip you up.

Sensei played with her eyes cast down. She didn't make jokes or chat when I stopped to make notes but sat silently waiting for me to finish, her pick mid-air.

During one of these sessions, I asked what was wrong.

"Not so comfortable. No feeling, this piece. I don't like. Are you OK, enough?"

The atmosphere of the room became so throttled when we played "Plum Ballad" that I gave up and never asked her to play it again.

When I think of my vocabulary notebook I think how ironic, the Munch portrait, and that I remember it now, when talking about the drums, when time began to go haywire inside me and a violence rose up that made me feel I could kill something.

There were words in the notebook that she had used to explain Japanese society. *Inshitsuna:* "the unpleasant corners of experience, insulated and ingrown." *Anmoku no ryokai:* "without words, we have to understand." And a popular saying about child-rearing in Japan: *Ame to muchi:* "You know, Janet, candy and the whip."

Perhaps it was she who wanted to scream.

≡

I found Kikuyu-sensei, right away, very cool. Sitting at the long low table smoking Kool cigarettes, punctuating her raspy speech with kabuki phrases like *Sorewa sorewa,* "Well, well," and *So nan da,* "Exactly right." She loved mischief, and tortured her friend, Kihiro-sensei the singer, by intentionally singing a refrain of a different song from the one they were about to play. Because songs were so similar—someone once joked that only the lyrics changed—Kihiro-sensei would sometimes get things mixed up.

All drums had to pass through Kikuyu-sensei's hands first. It was a task that the player could do, of course, but it showed respect for Kikuyu-sensei, and was a ritual that started every lesson. She checked rope pressure and then dipped a finger into a teacup of water, as I'd seen Sensei do, and affixed a small piece of paper on the rear skin of the drum, dabbing at it with her ring finger and then breathing on it a lot. If it was still too dry, she'd add another layer of paper and more breath. When she was satisfied, she handed the drum back to the player, who would bow and thank her in long polite syllables. While all this was going on, her students emptied her ashtrays and gossiped. Kikuyu-sensei nodded, *So nan da.*

At drum lessons, the teacher sits across the room from a line of students, behind a tall wooden block called a *hyoshiban.* On this sturdy block she slaps the beats of several different drums with two leather fans—a feat of independent motion—and calls out drum patterns using oral mnemonics.

Arm positions had to be correct on the *taiko,* stick drum, as each height brought a subtly different tone. The drumsticks were to be held loosely, with only thumb and first two fingers, but doing so made them feel as if they were going to fly out of my hands. Finding the one-inch deerskin patch in the center of the drumhead was a challenge, and most of my strokes fell wide of the mark, landing with a thud that had none of the ringing depth of a proper hit.

I did a little better on the *tsuzumi*, hand drum. *Pom!* was a slap in the center of the skin, releasing a watery tone. *Ta!* was a hit to the corner of the head, near its lacquered edge, releasing a drier sound, and bruising my hand. With my left hand, I was to squeeze the ropes and release them at the precise moment the right hand hit the skin to release the sound.

As on shamisen, little advice was given on how to perform these technical tasks, and, accordingly, no reward when it was done correctly.

"Uchioroshi!" "Ukemitsuji!"

I watched Kikuyu-sensei's fans until my eyes teared, trying to will my limbs to absorb faster. But there was no logic, only disconnected drum beats. I resented being thrown in with no help or encouragement. I felt my face flush with embarrassment.

We were playing *Hinazuru Sanbasso*, an eighteenth-century New Year's dance, where the dancer embodies a crow flying through the rice fields.

"Do you understand?" Sensei broke in, translating for something Kikuyu-sensei was insisting. "This is a bird, quick and lively. Become the bird."

On tea breaks we rubbed shoulders and puzzled over beats. *Was that four beats or eight? What does the triangle mean in the score again?* Sensei sat apart, her hair a convenient curtain, tuning her drum and staring out the window.

I pestered her to ask Kikuyu-sensei questions. There was so much I wanted to know. How did she practice? What did she do to prepare for performance?

"She practices on the train in her head. She reviews her notes the night before."

I made a show of my love for Kikuyu-sensei's specialty, the *taiko*. I fawned over its sweet ringing tone and royal spare strikes. The other two drums—a lap drum and hand drum—were always in chatty tandem. The *taiko* player sat apart, waiting for its solo role.

I imitated Kikuyu-sensei on the drum line. *Yooooo! Hooooo!* I scrunched up my brow. "Why so angry?" Sensei said later about my "drum face." "Scary."

Kikuyu-sensei took note of my surefooted strikes. She approved of my bold *kakegoe* shouts.

I worked hard to become her favorite. I was first to collect her drums. She brought me little treats, things she had been given but had no use for: a cute wooden box, a kabuki notebook. I brought her things, too, but when I spoke to her of them, it was in the clipped speech I had learned from Yoshi.

Sensei told me I had to use formal speech to speak to her because she was higher in status, so I studied the long strings of syllables and learned how to put myself down while raising her up. Now I said things like, "I am so sorry, this is a stupid boring thing, but please accept it as a gift from me."

On Valentine's Day, Kikuyu-sensei showed up with a pair of pink 3D glasses, I had no idea where she'd gotten them, but while sending her off in her Toyota with her drums that day, she called me over to her window and gave them to me.

I didn't want to compare Kikuyu-sensei and Sensei but I did. Maybe I was trying to be important to Kikuyu-sensei, hoping Sensei would see how valuable I was. I was using my own power, in other words, by comparing them, playing them off each other. And this was the reason why you couldn't have two teachers, I think. Comparisons like this gave power to the student. And for this kind of teaching, there really could be no equivocating, no choosing. One needed the disciple's total attention and obedience. Comparison bled energy and power. Distracted from the total learning. That fall, Sensei's hold on me ebbed, some force waned, and a terrible thing entered my mind: doubt.

=

The drums we learned were imported from the older noh theater, many years ago, and they didn't fit into the music exactly. They added texture and a sense of movement. Chords and harmony weren't used in our music. To move forward you needed the warm honeyed beats of the *tsuzumi*, the dry tick of the *okawa*, the ringing *taiko*. These drums added a palpable misalignment. They fit by not fitting.

I agreed to learn partly because I knew it was part of Sensei's secret mission, the complete severing she was headed for, a group of her own. She bought the drum scores for the entire repertoire— she could only afford a few a month—and started puzzling her way through the complicated graphs and numbers with a hardly contained joy.

I couldn't afford a drum of my own, and so I used Sensei's. She had several *tsuzumi* by then, and she liked taking them apart, mixing and matching different sets of skins with different *do*, the lacquered bodies connecting them, to see which were the best pair. "These two can't get along," she said. "These two love each other." To practice *taiko*, I used an old Chinese drum and she an overturned pot from the kitchen with wooden spoons for sticks.

As on shamisen, she pointed out all of my mistakes, instead there were more here, and such a minimum of understanding on my part that often the correction made no sense.

"*Uchioroshi* timing … you need to wait," she said.

But I didn't know *uchioroshi* in the first place.

"Hold on," I'd say. "I made a mistake … "

"In the *uchikomi*?"

"I don't know what it is but your hand was low and mine was high. See, there," I said, stabbing the notation.

"It's high if the pattern continues, it's low if it's the end."

Then there was the chance that once I could actually play one of these patterns correctly she would say, "Plus one!" or "Minus one!" and draw my attention to an exception that unraveled the whole rhythm and I had to sort it out again.

Sometimes Sensei would sit back, ladle and spatula in hand. "One beat? Two beat? Doesn't make sense." Sometimes the notation was wrong. Each guild had its own family secrets. I sat helpless, unlike on shamisen, where I could help sort out a new rhythm.

"*Te re tsu ku* ... no wait, this is ... " Even a half hour of this was draining, unlike shamisen where we could practice for hours.

I pressed Sensei for clearer explanations and began to see that rhythm was not her strong suit. I could not help but compare her weak timid beats with Kikuyu-sensei's sure strikes. I didn't want to see her fumbling with the wooden spoons on the drums, looking pathetic, not *zeitaku* at all.

Never was I so inside the music and so lost. I became dizzy, exhausted, cranky. We sat, drumsticks and wooden spoons in hand, nearly arguing, my head splitting. Nothing helped, not the notation, a series of vertical columns of X's and O's with scribbled kanji I couldn't understand. Not even the American professor when he visited our drum lesson on a trip to Tokyo that year.

We met him at the Hachiko Exit of Shibuya Station, a hip spot on weekends to meet up with friends. Sensei had dressed Jane and me in kimono, saying it would honor his visit.

The professor was as tall and broad as a linebacker, with thick white hair, and aviator glasses. He mumbled more than spoke, rambling about how today's traditional music was faster than in the 1950s, when he'd traveled by steam train from Osaka to Tokyo, where he had started writing the only book in English on Japanese music.

At the *keikoba*, we ordered special lunchboxes and crates of *mikan*, clementines. We invited him to join our lesson, but he refused.

"Arthritis," he said. "I can't bear to hear myself play."

But from the sidelines where he watched our lesson, he burst out in whole verses of song.

While the other students took their lessons and Sensei played shamisen for them, Judy, Kenneth, and I took the professor out for an iced coffee at a nearby family restaurant. Kenneth asked questions about his dissertation. The professor scolded us for using scores instead of memorizing the music.

"If you keep using the notation, you will never become a drum. You have to use your instincts, not your brain."

We complained about the illogical drum patterns, how impossible it was to follow Kikuyu-sensei's fans.

"It's all in eight-beat patterns," he explained. "That's the *yatsu-byoshi*. To count!"

Tsu-ha-ha-i-yo-on was the first four beats, *tsu-ho-ho-to-ttan* was the last. When the beat fell on a *yo*, the call was *yo*; when it fell on a *ho* it was *ho*. Until then, I had not connected the isolated drum calls to any larger pattern.

"Of course, the patterns are not always eight beats," he said. "They might be two or twenty." That would explain the frustrating two- or three-beat codas tacked on at the end.

"The only trick is that you can't have everyone pausing at the same time. Look at the sliding doors, all over Japan. Do you have a Japanese-style house? Two or more doors are in these parallel tracks, and each door has to be the same size. But when the doors move, they are starting from different positions. Only at the end of the track can they come to an equal, parallel position. The drums do the same thing."

He began tapping beats on the tabletop.

"The drums all operate on this eight-beat pattern, but the secret is this: the first beats don't line up! The *taiko kashira* pattern"—he imitated the crossed-arm drumbeat—"starts on beat eight!"

I was parched for knowledge, for some clue to get control of these irritating drums, and yet I didn't want to know. Knowledge, Sensei always said, is powerful because you can never go back to un-knowing.

My refusal had to do with Conrad's Kurtz: the fear of ending up round the twist. To learn their intricacy and complexity meant to adapt fully, and something in me resisted. I would never use the counting system the professor showed us that day, even when it was being called out at lessons by Kikuyu-sensei as she slapped her fans coolly on her wooden block.

That same day, the husband of Kikuyu-sensei's friend, an amateur noh actor, appeared at our lesson. He waded through the party, which was now engrossed in their lunchboxes, Judy and I crying out at each new surprising delicacy, and began rifling through a stack of scores in the corner, picking up one, dropping it, choosing another, as if he couldn't make up his mind. Finally, he turned to us stiffly.

"*Gaijin san, ne,*" he said, referring to the three foreigners in the room. He didn't say *erai*, well done, or look grateful. "But can foreigners really understand Japanese music?" he asked.

"He wrote a book," Sensei piped up, introducing the professor.

Everyone silently chewed and stared into their lunchboxes.

"Technique maybe," said the actor, "but not spirit." He used the word *kokoro,* heart.

"Ironic then that it was an American who saved Japanese music, isn't it?" The professor's temper flared.

"Really?" Judy said.

"The Japanese government wanted to uproot it after the war, saying it couldn't contribute to the moral character of Japanese people like Beethoven could," the professor said.

"We had no other response after the war," the actor said.

"A young officer in the Occupation went to MacArthur to plead the case for preserving it."

"Really?" said Judy.

The actor squinted. "Six hundred years," he said and left.

This would explain old photographs of smiling Japanese faces greeting the Western victors after the war. Maybe they'd be happy we were restoring their music. Maybe it took an outsider to see its value first, before returning it to them, enlivened.

The second part of Sensei's ad had always baffled me. *Take something home with you from your stay in Japan!* Why didn't she encourage us to use it right here?

All my frustration focused around the drums. Their unlocatable rhythms, pieces of a puzzle that wouldn't fit, knocked around in my head until it ached. Underneath the fatigue, deeper down, I felt angry, almost violent, like if I didn't figure out this tangled snarl it would kill me. I would destroy or be destroyed. It was a life or death struggle. Ridiculous but that was how it felt.

At the time, all-you-can-eat buffets were popular in Tokyo. They were called "Viking," a barbarian stuffing of one's face, antithesis to Japanese meals of over forty ingredients delivered on trays of delicate bowls and dishes. "Primitive" was the word Sensei used that first day. Drums were more ancient and mysterious than shamisen. Tokyo felt like a charmed ancient civilization, despite its modernity. The base instincts, the inner urges, were cinched by the civilized self. It was the sublimation culture—the learning culture, people often said—through rigid impossible forms. All was process, all becoming. In the noh version of *Hamlet*, the Danish prince says, "To be or not to be is no longer the question, the readiness is all, the readiness is all…." People were shaped into being by forms. Bending to rules retrained their instincts, their inner wildness gone. Perhaps creativity was squelched because creativity required aggression. It took an act of violence to be born.

≡

When I talked to Alan on the phone, memories of the sunset *torii*, the waterways of the Inland Sea, returned. I reported everything I was doing and thinking. He told me about his family, his studies. On the phone, he came alive in ordinary ways: his voice, his laugh, his eager questions.

In letters, our passion flared. I dashed off missives at cafés between classes. When I found one of his in my mailbox, I'd slash open the thin blue aerogram, unfold it like origami, and read it fast. Then I'd sit and imagine Alan in one of his cardigans and corduroys, looking boyish and handsome, and I'd read it again slowly, and start my own letter on scratchy transparent sheets, stuffing them into the thin envelopes and pasting them with stamps.

Alan sent pictures of him standing with his family under a maple tree turned fiery red and gold, someone holding a football, people wearing sweaters and smiling. It made me long for the autumn of my hometown, the roads I once sped down at the wheel of my parents' car, tunneling through the golds and oranges and reds, heart pounding. I was driving down to south county, where the artists were, and my destiny, I could feel it, with these people up from New York, performing for us country folk. I passed hors d'oeuvres on silver platters at their parties in tuxedo pants and white shirts, but at the wheel of the car, I was in command.

In truth I was a reckless driver. I'd spun off the road more than once with friends in the car. After one solo accident I left the car and hitched a ride to my dad's barber shop. "You can't leave the scene of an accident!" he roared, calling the police.

How did he know that? How did I not know that? There was so much to learn that people didn't tell you. Did they assume I knew? Nothing was talked about or shared or discussed at home. And so when the pictures of Alan and his autumn reverie made me deeply nostalgic, it was confusing. What was I longing for? His autumn scene was not a scene I knew. No one in my family stood under the maple trees like that, with dogs and babies, in sweaters, playing football together.

Sometimes I complained to Alan about Japan.

"I sneezed the other day and everyone chimed, *Aircon byo! Odaijini!*—I just want to have my own goddamned cold." Or, "Lisa re-gifted my rice crackers souvenir from Nagano! I brought them for her, not the entire school!"

Such rants alarmed Alan. Why was he going to return if I was unhappy there?

If I complained about our situation—the long absences, the expensive telephone bills—he took it to mean I was criticizing him, and wasn't he just trying to provide for a future, one that included me?

I complained to Sensei. "The calls are so expensive. He won't tell me when he's coming back."

She squinted. "You don't think he is cheating?"

"No," I said, surprised. "He's not like that."

"Hmm ... but men ... common," she said.

For my birthday in December 1997 I went to Milwaukee to visit Alan. His mom reminded me of an old woman out of a German fairytale, in a wide-wale corduroy skirt, rag wool socks, and Birkenstocks. A hardy, solid Midwesterner, she was startlingly open, greeting me with vivid blue eyes and embracing me as if we were already in cahoots.

In the mornings, we puttered lazily at the kitchen table over coffee and strudel, the dog wandering in and out of his bed below. Talk lingered, there was no rush to clean up, no being whisked out of the kitchen to go get lost before dinner.

I wasn't who Alan thought I was, I worried. He didn't see the collapse after he left Japan, the tears, the helplessness. *Who was empty without a man anymore? That was the fifties!* He knew nothing of my American life, my family, that it wasn't idealistic at all, that I was riddled with conflict about it, that home, as Sensei's daughter had said during a fortune telling, "would always be a question with me."

Just before Christmas, Alan and I spent time at my parents' cottage on Cape Cod. One night we were sitting in front of the fire, sipping wine, when he handed me a small jewelry box. Earlier, that fall, he had sent me a video instead of a letter. In it, he got down on bended knee in his boyhood bedroom, and, looking straight into the camera, asked me to marry him.

In those days in Tokyo after the Inland Sea, we'd talked about it, but in a careless unreal way. I'd wear a white hood like in Shinto weddings! How many kids? We hardly knew each other. In our letters we revealed our private thoughts, but we had no experience of everyday ordinary life.

Now I said to myself, taking the box, Love will prevail! Life be damned!

I squeezed open the box to find inside, on a bed of blue velvet, a silver pendant of a wedge of Swiss cheese.

I was now an honorary Cheesehead, he joked.

He was tying me to his life from before. It had to do with making a future, I see now. But something in me closed along with the box as I let him fasten the cheese around my neck. There was no money, he said. No way to marry now, with him in school. He needed more time. Another semester. Then he'd join me in Japan.

When I got back to Tokyo, Sensei encouraged me not to think too much about Alan, and was shocked to learn that we wrote every day and talked on the phone several times a week. I don't know if the shock was financial or if being tied to Alan meant to her becoming a dutiful wife. She said when he came back we should get separate apartments. She faced her palms out. "Side by side."

I couldn't imagine such a thing. On the phone with Alan, I acted like the independent, breezy expat he'd fallen in love with. But after my visit home, I had no idea what his intentions were, nor mine. I also had no notion of where my music was going. I could see only a long road ahead, with Kenneth's backpack and Sensei's obi in front of me, their destinies entwined with my own. I was embarrassed that I didn't know more about their situation or try to find out.

I was pained most by the translations. With Kenneth Sensei had begun taking down a small square green leather-bound book that I longed to be able to read. It contained all the *nagauta* pieces, all the stories they contained, historical notes, musical commentary. Everything I wanted to learn was in that one book, it seemed then. She opened it and read, stopping to think, translate, and Kenneth took pages of notes, and typed up translations with footnotes at the bottom.

Sensei called this, excitedly, "brain work." I don't think she ever saw herself as a scholar. When she later took a correspondence course at a place called University of the Air—I would find her in the mornings in a quilted *hanten* jacket, sitting sidesaddle at an antique desk on the floor, a long sharp pencil in her hand—she called it University of the Airhead.

Sometimes I felt nowhere, and to land for a moment I called Yoshi, just to go for coffee, or a walk around in shops, or have a drink, and then, I wouldn't want to, but I would touch him in an aisle, knowing how he would respond, and we'd end up at a love hotel, or once, a station bathroom, pressed into a stall.

I only did it a few times. I told no one. I think it was the secrecy that I needed.

My own life.

11

... a kind of unhinged moment ...

That winter, Sensei's mother in Toyama fell ill. She took Kenneth with her on the long train rides over the mountains to the sea, to continue the translation work. "Good distraction," she said. I wanted to go with her, to see the place of her childhood, where the snow made drifts so high people built staircases from second-story windows, and where a *shinkiro* appeared, a mirage, when the coastal fog and mist were just so.

I assumed it was cancer. She never said. Disease was rarely discussed in Japan, least of all with the patient, for fear it would negatively affect the time they had left. Sensei described her mother's illness with the Japanese aesthetic *jo-ha-kyu*, beginning-middle-end. In late January, she declared, "She is now *kyu* stage. Out of my control."

Kenneth escorted her to the funeral. I stayed behind in Tokyo, where twelve inches of snow fell, as if from a mistaken cloud destined for somewhere else, causing unheard of drifts to close businesses and hold up traffic. Girls traveling to shrines for the Coming of Age Ceremony ditched wooden clogs and resorted to platform boots under their long-sleeved kimono. On my street people tied plastic shopping bags over their shoes and went out to clear the snow with brooms and dust pans. The shrine down the street was dusted in white, its stone lanterns wearing hats of conical powder.

I tried to picture Sensei's snowy hometown of Toyama. I wondered what Japanese hospitals looked like, what the funeral entailed, and how Kenneth would know what to do. The long train journeys to her mother's bedside were maybe a way for Kenneth to give Sensei something, to pay her back for all she had given him. Maybe she needed him, too, to tether her to her life in Tokyo as she reached back into a painful past.

I wondered what their relationship was, what Kikuyu-sensei and the housewives at drum lessons thought. Music was their bond; anything further was a mystery to me, like her job, the evidence of which I saw only in her occasional mention of "jail," her rising hour of 4:30 a.m., her hosiery and slips spinning on laundry hangers on the veranda.

She made our music books on her lunch hour, photocopies of her original scores, which were on cheap yellowed rice paper from after the war. I pictured a cafeteria with tables and benches. Where was the photocopier? Who did she sit with? She sometimes mentioned practicing flute. Where? In front of everyone? Or did she go to a little nearby garden or dirt-packed park to sit alone on a bench?

From time to time a wet hunk slid from a tile roof with a soft plop, but otherwise the streets of Tokyo were filled with silence.

=

Sensei returned from the events in Toyama unchanged, the black hair perfectly cut, her small figure leaning over a bowl of rice in the kitchen. The only difference was the absence of music. For a week after the funeral, she rolled the music table into a corner and sat instead with Sasaki-san in the middle of the music room surrounded by stacks of kimono. Silk, wool, striped, padded. Stage robes with long skirts, formal wear for funerals and weddings, casual wear to visit the grocer or clean the house. This was a life spent in kimono— a life Sensei rejected—in boxes and boxes now arriving at her door from Toyama, an unexpected avalanche, like the snows.

Sasaki-san was her trusted—and very handsome—local antique dealer who gave her first refusal on old shamisen that came into his shop. Together they hovered over his finds like mechanics under the hood of a car, determining value, damage, what could be saved.

Sasaki-san worked his way through the piles of robes, commenting on variety and sleeve length. Aside from a few that Sensei would keep to wear and or make into instrument covers, they would all be sold. "Too small for you. Too bad," she said.

He combed through the piles and came up with a figure for the lot. Sensei agreed. Then she slid one out, untied the thin knotted string of the wrapping, and opened the soft paper to reveal a cream organza silk with an orange landscape of plum branches and swallows. It was a child's long-sleeved robe, from a dance performance or a shrine visit.

"Do you like?" she asked me.

The silk was stiff and smelled faintly of incense.

I nodded.

She fetched her surgical scissors, and with one stroke of the eight-inch shears, sliced through the sleeve.

It was the perfect size to make the pouch that covered the sound box of the shamisen.

"Please make yourself," she said, handing me the dismembered sleeve, adding a plain blue swatch for a lining. She had always made them for me, working at her tiny sewing machine in a sun-splashed corner of her rooms on a weekend morning.

I still have the material somewhere. I have never quite trusted myself to make it.

=

Sensei then did things then that I didn't understand but chalked up to grief, to a kind of unhinged moment. Reason didn't enter into it.

She gave away many of her mother's things, even to new students, strangers who just came in the door, maybe even just tourists, there for an afternoon. I don't know how she made the choice, what her qualifications were for recipients of the wrapping cloths, dance fans, and tiny tabletop gold screens that had been in her life for decades. Perhaps that was the point: you gave first, worthiness followed. Or perhaps this new small loss was a distraction from the larger one.

She gave her mother's shamisen to Kenneth. I tried hard not to feel like I deserved it, tried not to wants its glossy black wood and genuine cat skin etched with a faint marking from her mother's pinky. What she gave me was not practical but of rare beauty: a dance fan commissioned by her mother. Its bamboo ribs were lacquered a rich caramel color that creaked when opened. On one side of its gold paper was a modern painting of cherry blossoms. On the other side, the face of a geisha.

One afternoon I stopped by, and after a meal, Sensei and I lingered in the music room. The music table was still not parked back in the center of the room, there were no shamisen or scores set out. Instead, she got the idea of dressing me in her mother's robes. She installed them around the room, like portraits in a gallery. My favorite was a long-sleeved robe of burnt orange with scattered red, white, and green maple leaves at the top. Mid-robe was a bridge and greenery, and at the hem, royal blue swirls of water with a few floating leaves "fallen" from the top. Wearing it was like becoming an autumn landscape.

Sensei draped the robe over my shoulders and I felt my way into the sleeves.

"Play," she said, handing me a drum.

We tried another robe. I faked a flute.

"So gorgeous," she said.

Not me, I think, the kimono, the instrument, the landscape of beauty around her.

=

That spring, on a Saturday afternoon, Sensei and I were sitting in the kitchen. She was tapping a *tsuzumi* at her shoulder, several times lowering it to her lap and, with thumbs, gauging the rope pressure.

Sometimes she unknotted and tightened the cord all over and tried from the beginning to make a sound.

I had recently seen the actors from our show *Canton* in Shibuya. They said they were putting on Mishima's noh play *Dojoji* and had the idea of using traditional Japanese music. Would we be interested?

The drum at her shoulder made a dry shallow sound.

"You're always talking about expanding shamisen music," I said, pouring hot water for tea. "This could be a perfect opportunity."

"But music should be main."

"You could direct it all, tell us what to play and when. It could be really effective."

"I have no experience. I don't know best way."

Unsatisfied with the sound, she lowered her drum and began again to tighten its ropes.

"I have the script in Japanese," I said, bringing two steaming tea cups to the table. The tea was a fine grade of *sencha*, a winter gift from her teacher. "Will you look at it?"

Sensei put the drum in her lap and changed the subject. "I was pregnant with Tamami the year Mishima committed suicide. My teacher had just lost his first wife, and later same year his teacher died. It was very heavy time. Every day my husband was stealing my train money to gamble on horses. He came home drunk. I hated him. It wasn't fair, that he lived and so many talented people died."

She scooped up the drum and settled it on her shoulder again. The pattern on the lacquered body was a seashell. The patterns were sometimes a pun by the maker to refer to the sound it would make. Did this one mean the roar of the ocean? A deep sound? A distant one?

"This *do* has never made a sound," she said, taking it down and relacing again. "But with this skin, it finally found a good partner. It can take a long time to find a match. I'm happy. How long is my life?"

"The play is about beauty," I said.

She put the drum on the floor of the empty middle room and came back to the table. She sipped her tea and reached for a rice cracker. After a few thoughtful chews, she tilted her head.

"Maybe good idea. Kelly needs a chance to perform."

"Kelly?"

Kelly was her latest student, a nineteen-year-old from Moose-jaw, Canada. Sensei had called me after his first lesson to do her preliminary armchair psychologizing. "Canadian," she said, listing nationality first, which rankled me, as did being listed in concert programs by first name only, as if all foreigners were Cher. "His parents are musicians. So gorgeous."

When I met Kelly the week before, he had brought a spare tee shirt to cover the profanity on the one he was wearing. "I like to make noise," he said. He played well but seemed dissatisfied with the unamplified strum of the shamisen. He wanted louder, meaner, screechier. "Is anyone doing anything new with shamisen, like scraping noises?"

Sensei broke a rice cracker and popped a piece into her mouth. "So talented person, Kelly," she said. "Maybe he knows the play."

For the rest of the evening, I plied her with questions about the drum, the skin, the *do*, questions I knew the answers to but asked anyway. When she handed me the drum, I took the soft hemp ropes in my fingers and raised it to my right shoulder, tapping gently. A liquid tone traveled through the wooden body at my ear. I was careful. I knew that one tap too rough and the surface would split.

=

The noh play *Dojoji* was the same story I had seen at the kabuki, about a woman in love with a priest who goes to the temple, traps him under the bell, and turns into a snake ghost. In Mishima's updated version, a young modern woman interrupts an auction where rich people are bidding exorbitantly on an exquisite chest. She says it is only worth ¥3,000 and begins to relate the object's haunted history. The wardrobe belonged to a couple whose wife kept her lover hidden inside. The husband, hearing noises, shot through its doors, killing the man. The dead lover had once been the young woman's lover, too. But he ran away from her to be with the rich wife, she says, choosing secrecy, fear, and uneasiness over a happy life of love. The woman thinks he ran away from her beauty. If she were old or ugly, she says, he would have stayed. Like the wardrobe, an article only acquires value when old and obsolete.

As rehearsals began, it was refreshing to see the actors. Kenneth and I reminisced with them about *Canton*, making our old pun on *ohayo*, the greeting "Good morning," with Ohio. Sensei brought tea to the music table, which she had lowered so we could sit around it on floor.

Kenneth sat on one side of Sensei, I on the other. Sensei kept her eyes low, nodding at the director's comments. I could not understand the whole conversation, only *muzukashii*, "difficult," and *yoku wakaranai*, "I don't really get it." I recognized a mood between the fury of the snow globe and the playful geisha of the music room. It was the mood of a sulky adolescent. She kept her head down, seemed overly literal while also in a kind of fog, and asked, "Wh—what?" a lot, as if the questions were too hard for her to hear. Explaining over and over exhausted me, which was maybe the point.

Finally, we decided on some musical excerpts, including a fast solo for the moment when the young woman dashes into the wardrobe with a vial of sulfuric acid, threatening to disfigure her face. The actors envisioned strobe lights. Kelly would love it.

Sensei was shocked at the theater, a simple black box on a back street of Shibuya lined with pink azaleas in the May sunshine. There was no red carpet or folding gold screen, only an industrial-version pine tree made of twisted steel. She disliked having to play several shows, especially Saturday, which included a matinee. We sat on chairs against the back wall blending in with our formal black robes. I bought one for the occasion with a generic family crest since I didn't have one.

At the end of the play, the woman decides not to destroy her face. She exits the wardrobe, and her own youthful beauty is echoed by the height of spring around her. Inside, she had realized that all her suffering, jealousy, anger, and pain at losing her lover had not changed her face. She becomes resigned to nature, not fighting it anymore. "Nothing that happens can ever change my face."

The show sold out. My Japanese teacher came. I had passed a national language test with her help that winter. We stood outside after, talking with friends. They loved the show and spoke of its themes of beauty and redemption. I laughed into the camera, trying not to notice Sensei standing darkly by the van, waiting to be driven home.

When we got to her rooms, we ate quickly while she did a load of laundry. Unlike her concerts, where we pored over the videos, reviewing highlights for weeks afterward, we did not speak of *Dojoji* again.

≡

In July 1998, after the damp oppressive rainy season, we had our drum recital. It was nearly a year after *Canton*. "*Irrasshai!*" Kikuyu-sensei greeted us warmly at the performance space, a seaside hotel in Kamakura. She told Kenneth, Judy, and me to look around the town and have a swim at the beach later.

Sensei hadn't wanted to perform there. "They are all housewives. We have to pay."

But I had insisted. I was furious that our lessons might be for nothing, and I wanted a chance to impress Kikuyu-sensei.

Sensei dressed Jane and me in identical *yukata*, cotton summer robes of traditional white and navy blue. After I was dressed, I walked around tapping out drumbeats. Unlike for Sensei's shows, Kikuyu-sensei expected us to memorize our parts. I looped around again for each song, fiercely connecting the notes, burning them into my fingers. When to enter. When to exit. Just don't miss a beat and the *kakegoe* will be perfect.

We were playing *tsuzumi* for the pieces *Sanbasso* and *Goro*. Only one person could play *taiko* at a time. I played it for *Suehiro*. The order of the day was traditional. The recital would go on all afternoon, with professional musicians coming and going, up until dinnertime, when they would nod, bow, collect envelopes of money, and head for the train to go home.

We kneeled in the front row for our songs. The drummers were always out in the front, exposed. I'd spent many a concert in the front row staring at them, watching the sweat bead up on their brows.

Being in front now I felt a new kind of nervousness, but a new confidence, too. Unlike the shamisen, I didn't have to worry about a sweaty palm catching on the shamisen neck as it tried to slide along, or the shamisen slipping off my lap in kimono. I liked sitting idle for a long time, and I liked the dramatic approach to the drum: a slow sliding apart of the hands, one hand reaching for the drum and bringing it to the lap, the hot breathing on the back skin, the private affair of tuning it and readying it for sound.

Suehiro came first as a celebratory good-luck piece. *Sanbasso* was somewhere midway through and then a little later was *Goro*, where Jane and I were on hand drums, looking no doubt *kawaii*, cute, in our matching robes. Kenneth was playing flute, but not solo. Next to him was a professional Japanese flute player who called herself Pat.

We set off into the sea of notes. The song was very familiar by now. The opening guttural drawl pulled the shamisen into a frenzied ostinato. The melodic choruses began to sweep up and down over the shamisen's trusty footsteps. The tuning changed to *ni agari*, all sweetness, a flute entered as on a breeze, and Jane and I raised our drums to our right shoulders to start our duet.

Shamisen plinked. Singers swirled. But then, as sound accumulated, and we were in the *chirashi*, all sound colliding as it was supposed to before the final paring away, something shifted. Jane and I kept going but our drumbeats didn't match. Had we gotten off rhythm? Did our counting fail? The song got bumpy, the melody unraveled. Time lost its footing and it seemed, for a moment, like all sound might stop. Pat's flute went silent and I heard Kenneth's softer stream still going. Judy and I kept slapping at our hand drums. Finally, the singer and shamisen returned and we came together as the final cadence tumbled out.

The stage was a large tatami room with no curtain. At the end, we rolled off our knees and murmured polite phrases. I turned around to look at the shamisen and singers behind me to see what had happened. There was Kihiro-sensei, the woman who had sung beside me in *Goro*. She was doubled over in laughter.

I looked for Sensei who was listening and said something briefly. "Was she apologizing?" I asked.

"Of course not," she explained. "Kihiro-sensei went into another song."

"What?"

"Kikuyu-sensei must have been teasing her. In *chirashi* section, she went into *Hanami Odori*."

I expected she would be furious about the error, about someone tampering with the purity of the music. If she was, she betrayed none of it, padding to the off-stage area where the housewives, "dragon ladies," waited. They kept their drums in hard cases so they didn't have to assemble them from scratch, like Sensei did every time, carrying hers in silk pouches she sewed from stiff silk obi. These women wore prefolded obi. All they had to do was fasten it on their backs. They did not stand in front of the mirror with seven feet of silk at their feet, winding it round and round so that it would end at the precise length, tying it in front while you assembled the rest of the silk in a flat bundle at your back.

Sensei hated kimono and yet this is how she did it. There was no "good enough." You couldn't, after rounds and rounds with the silk and folds say, "Oh, that's not quite right, but it'll be fine." You unraveled the whole thing and started again. She didn't want to simplify anything, in other words. Music was not a hobby, and it was not a job. It was purer to her than that. And this sometimes infuriated me. It was like she made things harder on herself, not easier.

Before our performance I had come upon her sitting against a wall reading a book. Women around her were gossiping and snacking in groups. She looked like a statue in a dancer's pose, her legs in kimono sidesaddle next to her, a tiny slip of skin above her tabi showing. Her hair was oiled and combed perfectly into its implacable helmet. She was beautiful and remote.

The sight of her alone upset me. She had no one but us.

"Why don't you try to get along with anyone, make friends?" I wanted to say. I had no honest idea, no insight into what her life was really like, why she was the way she was.

It's not safe, I wanted to say. Don't trust us. We will leave.

I hated her because I couldn't face the fact that I had started thinking about that, too, sometimes when looking at those pictures of Alan, with the wool sweaters and football games. Instead, I went to her and we spoke together in English, isolated from the women around us. We talked of concerts and lessons and the little kabuki book she was reading. It was if we were in the snow globe together now, all unreasonableness and petty greed far away.

On the beach afterward under the open sky I looked out at the curve of the hills and gathered broken seashells, deep gray scallops with pearled purple in their fanned ridges, shells that, in the past, I would've thrown back because they were broken. Now I felt lucky to possess such a sliver of beauty at all.

12

… coil, rupture, repair …

Other things were changing that year in ways I couldn't have imagined. I learned to walk like a woman. Bending the knees slightly, back straight, I glided in sock feet from one corner of the stage to the other.

"Don't pop up like that!" yelled Tachibana-sensei, sitting at a low table in the next room. "Stay low. Smaller steps! She is soft, eh?" I heard her say to Seiko, the young woman sitting next to her, waiting for her turn. Seiko ran a jewelry stall by the station and was a fan of our shamisen gigs. She had flagged me down one day as I was passing with an elegant turn of her wrist.

"Janet-oh! I am dancing again!"

Before long she had brought me, too, to Tachibana-sensei's two-story house behind the 7-Eleven to learn the unbearable pain of Japanese dance.

The female dances are about containment. In them you burrow deep in, like *okusan*, wife, literally "the person at the back of the house." All dance students start with female dances because it is harder to coil inward, to become as small as possible. A geisha can perform an entire dance on one two-by-four-foot tatami mat. It looks like she is just dawdling along, biting a hand towel and swooning, but it is not a hapless arrangement. She is following strict rules: allowing her body to only appear at a diagonal, making a pleasing S-curve of her collar and sash. Her feet are aslant, never forward. The dance is a combination of movement and stillness. The point isn't to keep moving, but to start over and over from a place of stillness. You don't hide the pauses, in other words. They are part of the flow. Coil, rupture, repair.

It was a transition I was seeking out that year, the passage from one place to the next. Years later, when I was visiting Sensei, I was complaining about how hard it was to go back and forth. She never saw the havoc of my life, how desperately I wanted this coming and going, and how much I thrashed against it.

"Hard, transitions … " she said, nodding. "Because you have to take responsibility."

=

Tachibana-sensei was encouraging. She watched me as I danced and gave constant feedback, rushing in to fold an elbow or plant me more squarely on my feet. *Koshi o irete,* she said, straightening my hips until they were parallel to the floor, my leg muscles shaking. The dance revolved around the *koshi*, solar plexus. She'd then back away and I'd try to remember the pose by the exact location of the pain.

Fortunately, a lesson was only about fifteen minutes, half hour tops, and ended with a low bow to each other, fans closed before us, in the middle of the stage. After my lesson, I watched Seiko's, and then the three of us smoked and drank tea and gossiped.

Tachibana-sensei smoked lushly, stabbing a long Virginia Slims into her plastic filter and puffing on it with her brightly painted lips. She was pretty, with a wide face and cheekbones and bright eyes. Her rooms were bright and airy, unlike the brown linoleum and hooded gloom of Sensei's fluorescent lights. Tachibana-sensei smiled. She was upbeat. And she had a husband. When he came home at night, she revved up the fans to clear the smoke and told us to wait while she brought "papa" his dinner tray. I had formally met him when I started, as if he had to know who was spending time under his roof. He didn't say anything much, only hello, in the darkened room where he sat in front of the TV.

When I told Tachibana-sensei about Sensei, she plugged her filter with a new cigarette. *"Erai, ne ... nani ryu?"*

What school? she wanted to know.

And then I had to explain that there was no school, my teacher wanted to keep the music alive, and so on. Tachibana-sensei said she herself had been born and raised in *shitamachi*, the old town of Tokyo. She was the real thing, she assured me, clamping the lipstick-stained filter between her teeth.

"She teaches for free," I said.

Her eyes got wide. "Free? *Mezurashii, wa!*" she said, Rare! adding a feminine *wa* to her sentence, which Sensei never did.

Because I knew the music so well by now, I was a confident beginner. Tachibana-sensei praised me often and prided herself on anything I learned. She was always amazed at how soft I was, how I would make the movements even if they were totally wrong. I tried. I had no shame.

"But she's a housewife," Sensei complained when I told her about dance lessons with Tachibana-sensei. "Rich husband. Easy for her."

"I know, but it's really helping my sense of rhythm on the shamisen...."

Sensei was at a loss as to what to do. She couldn't forbid me, so she just ignored it, as if I had taken up flower arranging.

Twice a week, I arrived at Tachibana-sensei's door and slid an envelope of money across the mats, feeling their cool softness under my palms. She taught me how to dress myself in a cotton kimono for my lesson, and I bought new tabi with five hooks, one hook higher than usual to hide the ankle during the steps. I also bought a nylon split underskirt so my legs could move under my robe. I was learning a brief interlude from the dance *Fuji Musume*, "The Wisteria Maiden." For an hour a week I was a girl viewing blossoms or Mount Fuji, her fan opening to create the tall flat cone in the distance, or to hide her innocent face.

After lessons, Seiko and I washed the stage by pushing damp rags across the floor, butts in the air while Tachibana-sensei changed and cooked. She brought us gooey rice pan-fried in soy and wrapped with seaweed. Miso soup stuffed with *asari*, littleneck clams. *Mama no aji*, she said, "mama's taste," as she brought the tray out and sat down in her blue jeans to eat.

The best part was that, walking home in the fresh night air with my bundle, passing the 7-Eleven, the karaoke bar, the darkened shrine in the distance, I was free to go. Tachibana-sensei was not someone I would want to be tied to. Her own dance was to *enka*, syrupy ballads. Her laughter was coarse, her chatter mindless. I thought dance would help me stay with Sensei and be free of her at the same time. I had already started practicing how to leave.

=

New columns of words appeared in my Japanese notebook, practical ones like LEFT RIGHT FRONT BACK DIAGONAL. I rode the trains standing without holding on to strengthen my *koshi*. I took the stairs to build up my legs. I swapped kimono and accessories with Tachibana-sensei late at night on her stage, buried in the robes like girls with our Barbie dolls. She suggested buying a made-to-order through her tailor so my sleeves would be long enough at lessons. I chose black pinstripe because stripes were sophisticated but casual, with an informal *komon* pattern of tiny red and white fans.

Tachibana-sensei taught me how to tie the kimono on myself. The hardest part, the obi, she showed me could be tied in front in the *cho cho*, butterfly, knot and then swiveled around to the back when done.

Dance was *kurushii*, hard, and I saw now why my students who, when injured, would never ask to be taken out of a sports match. They persisted in pain, myopia, and failure because to give up was the worst. Their *gaman*, a prized stick-to-it-iveness. I rooted myself to the floor at Tachibana-sensei's, finding a place of my own, moving to shamisen plinking from a tinny speaker in the corner of the stage.

At Sensei's I continued to practice the capo part for Kenneth's evaluation recital, his *benkyo-kai*. Sensei had to play in the lowest tuning because of his singing pitch, where the strings were slack and it was hard to sound bright and flirtatious. She also inserted many more vocal cues to make sure he got all the nuanced interplay with the shamisen. She started looking tired.

"Why don't you take a break?" I asked. "You've probably got it down by now."

"Kenneth needs me," she said.

Soon after, her teacher was passed over for status as a *ningen kokuho*, Living National Treasure, a title bestowed on living masters of Japanese traditions. It went to his nemesis instead, a singer we all disliked. Sensei rang out her usual pleading about Japan. "It's not fair."

The recital was held a few weeks after our drum recital on a stage in a geisha hall in Asakusa. Several were in attendance that day, marveling at Kenneth's voice.

Sensei's teacher, Kikuoka-sensei, sat before the stage in formal kimono, taking notes at a small desk. I'd never seen this before, only the yearly recitals that were like weddings in their elaborate months-long preparations and expense. After the performance Kikuoka-sensei would tell Kenneth everything he did wrong, like the Queen after the museum concert.

Sensei looked pained and shadowy, tenser than I'd ever seen her, with no inkling of pleasure or release. Coiled in her black robe, she looked like an ink blot at his right arm.

Kenneth looked tense. To his left was the capo player, imported from Hiroshima and the best in Japan. I had tried imitating her notes with a tape and gave up. The quality of her capo playing was extraordinary. There was nothing pinched about it; it was tight but loose and playful. I knew it would take years to play it like that.

The shamisen and voice interplay was so subtle, so delicate. To master it took not only skill but empathy, a feeling for what the other was doing, so you could anticipate it. To master these arts my student Etsuko had once said, "They are wife training, to learn obedience and duty." To twine your life up with someone else's until it was no longer just yours.

Sensei's *kakegoe* were like little whispers, or pillow talk, it almost seemed, from cushion to cushion. She was a geisha after all, it struck me, cuing him so he wouldn't fail, so that he would feel like a success. Not only to Kenneth but to me, too.

Dance was a way to keep moving, if pained, through Sensei's world. I wanted not to lose her, but I wanted a different relationship. I wanted her to be my teacher. To see in me what was there and nurture it to success. That she hadn't made me desperately fear that there was nothing to nurture. I had given her no money, only time, and devotion. I had nothing to offer her in return for her devotion, no position, no future academic standing, no status.

I was hedging my bets. In the event that I lost her permanently to Kenneth, that she followed him with her songs and strings, then I could still be with her in the dance, sliding a foot across the stage, pausing, tilting the neck, gesturing with a fan. Then I wouldn't lose her completely.

After the recital we stood outside in the sun and took pictures. Some of the geisha joined in, as did Seiko, who had come to cheer on Kenneth, who was tutoring her in English. It was thanks to him that she had returned to Japanese dance.

≡

How and when I found Yukiko I can't remember. How and when the Japanese student came to Sensei's rooms, I can't remember, either. But both events pushed our relationship into a place that became intolerable.

There were other happy musical events at the time. We invited a shamisen inventor and amateur singer to lunch and played songs so he could sing. We played shamisen at cherry blossom time on a blanket under some trees in a nearby park. The handyman returned with his wife and teenaged son to listen to us play. The boy, about to head to Germany for schooling, begged Kenneth to teach him flute.

Sensei named her group the Daita International Nagauta Kai.

We would perform that autumn at a community center, two years after my first performance singing. We invited a ventriloquist to perform during the intermission. Most of the guests came by word of mouth through Kin-san, Kenneth's elderly landlord, a futon seller.

But I couldn't help but think about Sensei's mission. Ever since *Dojoji*, I wondered if her way was the best one for carrying on this music. Rushing to get temporary students onstage, excerpting pieces, taking them out of context—would that really ensure its survival?

Yukiko was a new student in my class at the English school. Like Japanese schools, we started the year in April. Right away, she stood out from other students. When I asked questions, Yukiko would say, "Well, if we look at it this way ..." and spin some theories of her own while her classmates used the time to check their Tamagotchi, handheld digital pets, or slip in a round of Tetris, digital tile puzzles everyone was wild about.

Yukiko was a performer of modern dance and wore her long frizzy hair pulled up into a barrette on top of her head. She wore cowl neck sweaters and jeans, and high wedged heels to boost her height. She was tiny but had the energy of a whole classroom.

But she knew nothing about the traditional arts. When I told her I studied shamisen, she begged me to play it for her. Soon, she'd unlocked a ferocious curiosity about Japanese traditional performing arts. We went to torchlit noh plays under cherry blossoms, the famous actor Tamasaburo's *Fuji Musume* at the kabuki. And then she took me to a ballet by Béjart and told me about Mary Zimmerman's new interpretation of Medea.

After shows, we went to Pronto, a spaghetti café where she ordered *mendaiko*, noodles crowned with a nest of tiny orange fish eggs, and I ordered carbonara, a soupy bowl of noodles with ham and kernels of corn, and went over all the details of the show.

"The mask! What did you think, Janeto-sensei?" she would say. "It was like it changed completely. First it was weeping and then, just a little moving and it was something happy...."

She wanted to know about the shamisen, about *Dojoji*. She loved Mishima.

To earn money to go to the States she was working as a hostess. I was instantly dismissive and then envious. She had no puritanical history. Somehow I'd become so straitlaced. I envied her ability to separate out just a job needed to achieve her goals.

When I spoke of Yukiko to Sensei, she only nodded. *"Honto?"* "Really?" She didn't want to teach her or meet her. And when the first Japanese stranger, a young woman, answered Sensei's ad for shamisen lessons, she refused.

"I don't want to teach Japanese."

"But that's discrimination!" I said.

They wanted all the trappings of traditional culture, she said. Stage names, proximity to Living National Treasures, costumes, rituals, money.

"These kids go overseas and are asked about their culture and they don't know a thing," I said. "They can't share it or pass it on because they have no access to it. You could give them access."

I chose then to push an issue that was starting to weigh heavily on me.

"You could charge money for your lessons," I said quietly.

I was thinking of students who left after one lesson, sometimes with a shamisen in tow.

She shook her head. "Music is not about money."

The young woman wrote a vitriolic op-ed in an English weekly calling Sensei a racist.

"She doesn't know me. She doesn't understand my life," she said.

But when the next Japanese student called, a young woman who had just returned from New Zealand, Sensei accepted. I secretly hoped Tomoko would succeed.

For some reason, Sensei invited her to a drum lesson first. We were holding it at her house that week since the noh actor was having a recital on his stage, where we usually practiced. Judy, Kenneth, and I arrived in the late morning to set up the space. Kikuyu-sensei sat in the music room with her *hyoshiban* and we squeezed into a row in the empty room opposite her.

Tomoko entered and we all fell silent.

"Hai dozo," Sensei said, letting her in wearily.

Tomoko slipped out of her ballet flats and stepped up, introducing herself. Kenneth, Jane, and I said hello from the kitchen table where we were making notation booklets and talking about ways to combat the painful kneeling position by taping bandages onto the tops of our feet.

"Kawaii," she said of the cover I was making. I was suddenly self-conscious. Why was I pasting a copy of a score onto colored cartoon-like paper? Why didn't I buy original scores?

Sensei showed her into the rooms and led her to a floor cushion across from Kikuyu-sensei, who put out a cigarette and greeted her with a raspy hello. Sensei had all the doors to the veranda wide open to let out the smoke.

Tomoko looked at Sensei for what to do. Sensei said something. The girl bowed to Kikuyu-sensei.

I watched the lesson like a tennis match, my sympathy switching from one side to the other.

The girl's arm sagged weakly under the shoulder drum.

I know! It's so heavy, isn't it?

The girl casually struck the drum, handling it like an old sweater.

Careful! That drum skin is a hundred years old!

There was a pause in the lesson and I saw Sensei go to one of her drawers in the bookcase and return handing Tomoko a small nail clipper. She brought over the tiny trash can from her nightly hair-styling sessions.

After Tomoko was exhausted, the older ladies had their lesson, then us. By the time we came back into the kitchen, Tomoko had left, claiming she had an appointment.

At my next shamisen lesson, Sensei told me Tomoko quit.

"Drums? Shamisen?" I asked.

"Everything."

"But why?"

"She couldn't cut her nails."

I knew Sensei sometimes confused modal verbs. "You mean she *wouldn't* cut her nails."

Sensei shook her head. "Nail was attached to skin. Impossible to cut."

=

One might ask, Why couldn't I think for myself? Why couldn't I say, This isn't good for me, this doesn't work. Ask Sensei about it, reason it out. But, you see, she was my teacher, or something like it, beyond me, in that land of boundaried yearning, and it wasn't appropriate to ask. She had things I needed—the music, the shamisen—that I believed I could only achieve through her. And this feeling, I want to make clear, was not unpleasant. How often did I return in the ten years after I left Japan, and wake up in some small room in Tokyo to wash my face in cold water at the kitchen sink and stand amazed again at how quickly the kettle boiled, how plentiful the one cup of coffee filtering into a single cup. Every day was weightless at her side, without strands of the past. There was only this day, a kettle rustling, the last leaf on the persimmon tree ready to fall.

I would sometimes think, "I came back for this? A persimmon leaf? A bowl of sesame ramen?" And the answer was, "Yes."

What bothered me was that I might never shake this feeling of duty and inferiority. And what then? I'd always be that with her, doomed, as if inside her cape of hair, turning everything black.

Doomed because unrequited, as with Alan, with whom I could not seem to land on the same continent. The proposal was never mentioned again. I felt less engaged to Alan than I did to Sensei. Each semester, he deferred coming back. "Next term, I need more time." I didn't know how to say, This isn't working, I want more. I didn't know I deserved more, so I kept on, becoming cynical and edgy.

Out with a friend one night, I talked of Japanese gifts, that they were bribes to secure you in their favor, to bind you until you couldn't breathe. She was shocked. Me, who was so devoted?

Sometimes I wished Sensei would die. Then I could be at her

bedside, again the loyal disciple, with her daughters, who would translate the nurse's words and she would will all her music and instruments to me, and I would live on for her.

"When I die, probably Tamami will sell everything on eBay," she said once in her rooms.

It stung me that she didn't care, about me, about the instruments, about her whole world being sold off. It was like after the concerts when she would say, "It's over. Tomorrow is new life." It pained me that she could let go so easily and I could not. But then she would come back with a plan and I would rush to help, feeling all my limbs growing again, glad to still be alive.

≡

I made plans to move that fall. Seiko and her husband were divorcing and she moved out. I took a room in their house near the station, a Western-style condo with hardwood floors, skylights, and two dogs. Sensei was no longer responsible for my apartment. Things were changing.

One Saturday I was at a lesson with Kenneth. We were working on something new, a song he and Sensei had translated about an Edo dandy. During a break, I brought us a tray of tea and we sat sipping for a moment. Then Sensei broke the silence.

"I had to spend so much time this weekend washing all my *tsuzumi* ropes," she said. "I don't know who, some perfume or hand cream? Everybody has been using my *tsuzumi*."

I looked up at her but she did not meet my gaze.

"It takes thirty minutes to tie just one drum. I can't do. People should be more careful to wash hands."

"Maybe it was me. I'm sorry," I said. Kenneth was penciling something in his notation.

"So stinky," she said.

"If it was me, I'm sorry. I'll buy you new ropes. Just tell me where to get them."

We practiced some more, during which she pointed out every

mistake but didn't tell me how to correct anything. "No, nope," she said of my timing. "Go back."

I questioned her corrections but said nothing. After, she insisted we all go to Gusto, the "family commissary" next door. Sensei ordered her usual bowl of rice topped with raw tuna, Kenneth a hamburger steak, me the pork cutlet set. While she and Kenneth discussed the upcoming concert at the community center, I thought of my offense. With no chance to fix it, there was nothing to do but sit in wrongness and shame. The meal was endless. There was an odd mix-up where someone had switched the table top service bells so a waiter kept arriving at our table for no reason asking, "May I help you?"

We went back to her rooms to put everything away, wiping the long shamisen necks with velvet cloths and inserting their sound boxes into their layers of paper and plastic, and then the silk covers, tying them securely and hanging them back on the wall.

I walked with Kenneth as far as the path of cherry trees, now a steady blossomless green. We sat down on a bench and listened to the cicadas thrumming in the trees.

"Did you ever record them?" I asked. I knew he had recently been capturing sounds in Tokyo.

"Yeah, their call is different as they go through their life cycle."

"Seventeen years underground and one season of mating and death, right? Talk about unfair."

We laughed.

"Is everything okay with Sensei? She seemed really upset about the drum tonight."

I had never spoken to him of Sensei.

"I think she's upset at your taking dance."

"It's got nothing to do with her," I said, and then felt foolish. Of course it did.

"I think she thinks you're going to start asking her to play for your dance."

"I wouldn't do that."

"Don't worry. It's just a phase. She'll get used to it."

An awkward silence passed. I didn't ask him about the funeral or Toyama. I didn't know that I could.

"Check this out," he said, and reached into his backpack. He handed me a black and white photograph of a girl dancing "The Wisteria Maiden." She was lying in a languorous pose, a sleeve held to her lips, wearing the trailing padded kimono of a dancer, the white face of a geisha. From her heavy wig dangled a wisteria sprig.

I looked up. Kenneth nodded. "Sensei."

I peered at the photo again. She was gorgeous, an ancient beauty born into a world that survived only onstage. I wanted the photo instantly, as evidence of her trueness, her origins, her place in this world. She could have fit in, she could have had the life of a successful dancer or musician. Why did she not want to? Did she not have the skill? Was she not good enough? If she was, then to throw it away was a thing I didn't understand. What lay behind the picture was her history, the people, the house where she grew up. She had given these to Kenneth. She wanted him to hold onto her. She had given him the photo trusting that he would.

PART IV

13

… finally, he vanished altogether …

The night before a show everything rolled to a halt. Months of music practice, of writing of stage plans, of sending notes and emails, of watching Sensei sift through her students' weaknesses and devise ways to make them shine, of photocopying scores at 7-Eleven, of buying film and hiring cameramen, of gathering foods and kimono, all would pass, and after a brief dinner, Sensei would send me home, warning me of sidewalks and paper cuts. On these eves I would be lacing my shoes in the *genkan* and look up to find her inky eyes resting on me longer than usual. It always felt like goodbye, and in a way it was. The show upon us, we would now go our separate ways until after the performance when she'd ask me, *How did you go,* as if we'd been traveling and hadn't seen each other in a while. But the night before, my shoes laced, one hand on the door, her eyes seemed to want to pin us together in the moment before order was destroyed and chaos began. *Get a nice sleep, Janet.* She used my name. It always meant some kind of end was near.

Things started to unspool quickly in the fall of 1998. On a muggy day in late September, the powder blue tickets of Sensei's teacher's group appeared clipped to her lesson calendar. The routine was familiar by now. We arrived at the Marion building in Yurakucho in the morning with enough time to run to Subway for sandwiches and

Starbucks for coffees and a highly diluted latte for Sensei. It would be an all-day encampment of music, which we watched from the front row with our programs and recording devices, listening intensely. On the way home, I would hear the music in the ghostly peal of the train's brakes, the patter of feet on the station stairs. It took the whole journey just to leave the show.

Before the curtain we milled around the lobby. Sensei pointed out various characters noted for their skill or family, commenting on the unusual crowd.

"I think that's Sensei's brother-in-law," she said, craning her head to see.

The concert was a varied program that included a favorite of mine, *Azuma Hakkei*, "Eight Views of Edo," a sophisticated and highly technical composition with a shamisen solo that mimicked the sound of dyers pounding cloth on rocks in the river.

During the concert, Sensei kept looking around at the audience, vaguely restless.

"Strange. Ivora guy is here," she said at a break, referring to a shamisen inventor who built instruments out of eco-friendly materials—no skins, ivory, or rare trees. Sensei's teacher sometimes test-ran his inventions on stage.

"Maybe he wanted to hear the sound of his new pick," I offered.

"Of course not," she said, looking around the hall.

Sensei's teacher appeared in the finale, as usual, in the most difficult piece, *Adachigahara*, the story of two priests taming a female demon. It was one of the longest *nagauta* pieces, running over forty minutes. His playing was always the highlight of the show, and we eagerly settled into our seats to listen. How exposed shamisen performers were! How steady and surefooted their playing had to be, through fast solos that thrilled and constant tuning changes that refreshed. I leaned in, as if to inhale his mastery.

I had just begun to let out my breath after a particularly tricky passage when he stumbled with his plectrum. It was the tiniest slip, barely audible, and he didn't lose a beat, but it was there. Sensei had probably never heard him make a mistake in her life.

I didn't mention it after the show. We gathered our microphones and trash and headed for the door with the rest of the crowd. Sensei was silent.

≡

Kaze o hikanaide, ne, the Japanese say during the change of seasons. Don't catch a cold. No one just had the sniffles in Japan. Colds were ritualized. There were colds from the changing seasons; colds from the frigid air conditioning in summer; colds from falling asleep under heated tables in winter. Equally ritualized were the remedies: *okayu,* tasteless rice mush, or packets of powders from the pharmacist. *Odaijini!* was the ritual rejoinder. Take care!

After Kikuoka-sensei's concert, I came down with a nasty flu. My eyes and nose were in a perpetual drip. I ate nothing, but lay swaddled in blankets. I wanted to have my flu in peace, I did not want it absorbed into human experience.

One night, lying awake in my futon with a fever, I got a phone call from Tachibana-sensei. She was walking home from the train station, where she had just come from a day of visiting her mother in Ueno, the old part of town.

"Janeto-chan. Otenpura tabenai no?" She asked if I wanted some fresh tempura.

Sure, I said and got up to let her in when she arrived. *"Dozo."*

I led her into the main room of my apartment, apologizing for the futon, and gave her a floor cushion to sit on, staying away so as not to infect her. Tachibana-sensei offered up the tempura and two *manju* muffins stuffed with red bean paste. Her eyes widened as she gazed around the room.

"Sugoi wa ne. Nihonjin yori nihonjin da wa."

She was apparently surprised to see such a Japanese room. Sensei, too, often said I was more Japanese than the Japanese. I couldn't just be interested in tradition, it had to be an unusual phenomenon. I was tired of feeling freakish.

Her eyes landed on the dance fan from Sensei's mother, with the geisha face painted on gold paper. She went to see it and exclaimed at the reverse design of cherry blossoms.

"*Ii, ne. Mezurashii, kore.*" "How nice and unusual!" She offered to trade for it, as we did in our late-night kimono-swapping sessions.

I shook my head. "That was a gift from Sensei. It was her mother's."

Tachibana-sensei put the fan down quickly and sat down again to confirm our lesson schedule. After she left, Sensei called. She sounded quiet.

"I just got back from Sensei's house. He is sick."

The concert came flashing back—the relatives, the shamisen inventor, the mistake. I assumed this was not a casual illness. I would learn in time that it was accelerated pancreatic cancer. He refused Western medicine, only a trial of Chinese herbs. For years, Sensei had been getting him eye drops and sleeping pills for his insomnia because he hated doctors.

"I'm really sorry, Sensei."

We made arrangements for an upcoming rehearsal and I put the phone down and wrapped myself in the futon, shivering. I had met her teacher only once or twice in passing, and yet I knew him through Sensei's teachings. Rainy weather made for bad tuning. You could use a broken match stick for a capo. Learning came only through exposure to a master, slowly over time like a Polaroid coming into focus.

It was people who mattered in Japan. Even with the language barriers and cultural misunderstandings, there were people all around me in Sensei's world. People like Sasaki-san, rustically elegant in his white shirts and husky voice; the Kameya family of shamisen makers, whose owner came on house calls, unfurling his quilted bags of tools, oiled and worn with use; Kikuyu-sensei, Kihiro-sensei, the inventor, the handyman.

She supported so many people with her music: musicians, teachers, students, sheet music printers, *bachi* pick carvers, silk string makers, silkworm farmers, cutters and whittlers of rosewood and red oak; musicians she paid to see and kabuki actors, too, on their stages where she studied the music as it played out in riveting dance-dramas; the knitters who made the finger slings to slide along the neck, the people who made the dusting cloths to wipe down the neck after playing, carvers of the sandalwood and ivory tuning pegs; the rubber company that made the pads to keep the instrument stable on your lap, the person stitching the brocade covers for the sound box; the kimono makers of all the robes she bought for her students, the cheap washable ones and her own of antique silk; the stitchers of the obi sash, the silk weavers of the *obiage* scarf, the tabi makers, the *geta* clog makers, the hand-towel makers and dyers for the ones she tucked across her lap for more stability, the *bachi* glue to repair the patch of skin under the strings, and chickens for the eggs, for egg whites worked just as well; creators of cypress wooden boxes where she collected bridges and strings, makers of music stands and "cheater" chairs for sitting in *seiza* posture. (The only thing she didn't support very well were animals: cats and dogs, whose hides covered the shamisen in her room, and a couple of horse fetuses on hundred-year-old drum skins.) She brought all these people to me for little sips of experience. *Narau yori nareru.* "Absorbing" rather than learning.

I had never thought of the people living behind these things. With people, there were always complications. With people, it was never over.

I got up to turn off the light and caught the scent of Tachibana-sensei's perfume in the room, thin and hovering.

=

There were good days for us in Tokyo, and there were bad days, but for Sensei one of the worst might have been one day during the New Year's holidays of 1999 when she went to Kenneth's door. She might have had food from the international grocer down the street, or a request to practice. When she called me on New Year's Eve, when I was with Alan on Cape Cod watching revelers taunt the glittering ball in Times Square on TV, she recalled the incident like a detective.

"On December 30th at 2:00, new student, Ricardo came over
…"

She had been calling Kenneth but not getting an answer. Worried, she went to his door and rang the bell. What followed was eerily familiar to a story she had told me once that had to do with a drummer we saw often on the stage. I don't remember when she told me all this. But this story, it pervades all of my memories, echoing through our story together as I set it down now.

He and Sensei had once been engaged. Her mother loved him, she said. He was very handsome. Sensei was twenty-three or twenty-four at the time; he was older. He took her to his family in Kyoto and gave her a *tsuzumi*. It was a hopeful time, the late sixties. Japanese musicians were experimenting with new ways of playing music. Sensei was a student at the Fine Arts University. He was maybe a professional already. Around that time, a geisha in training entered the school. She had only a junior high school diploma, so she had to take a high-school equivalency test to apply to the school. She entered in April as a voice major.

That summer, Sensei's fiancé went home to Kyoto on break. On his return to Tokyo he failed to contact her, so she went to his apartment to try and find him.

"It was September 1st," she said. "They were together."

In bed, apparently, him with the geisha. She remembered a white face and hands.

She threw the drum he gave her into the trash. "Can you believe? I threw an instrument in garbage?"

She married her husband—"How do you say, rebound?"—and had her two daughters.

But she always remembered vividly walking in on them. It was like something out of an old movie. The woman put her clothes on—I can see tousled hair, bee-stung lips—lit a cigarette, exhaled, and said, "He's mine now. Go away."

=

Of Kenneth, Sensei now said, "He pushed me down the stair. Stinky guy. He was making sex."

Kenneth had come to the door in boxers with his hair messed up.

"He pushed you down the stairs?" I asked, signaling to Alan to turn down the TV.

I pictured her falling backward, horrified, from a great height.

"He tried to block door. He pushed me down the stair," she said. "So stinky. And stingy," she added. "He dumped our group."

"But why would he do that?" I asked. Kenneth was about to finish his dissertation, just barely making the ten-year deadline.

"He chose so wrong person. She's not even musician." This struck me as an odd thing to be thinking about. She was jagged on the word stinky, and stingy, struggling for more words. I could see her tiny figure pacing her rooms, the phone held loosely under her helmet of black hair, its ebony gloss darkening her face like a crow's wing. I wasn't sure which hurt her more, Kenneth leaving her music or his taking a lover.

"Do you know who it is?"

When she said the name, it all made sense. Who was the only woman I knew in the neighborhood who spoke English, who was interested in traditional arts, who was available? Seiko with the dogs and the jewelry stall—and my dance lessons—who was soon-to-be-divorced from her inattentive husband of many years.

"He destroyed everything," she said.

"You still have a group," I said. You still have me, I wanted to say. She was still giving him everything, even now, as she cursed his taking.

"Kenneth made the decision," I said. "He's an adult."

"And she's not even musical person. Women are demons, Janet." I could see the coal eyes in the fluorescent dusk of her rooms, flickering.

=

When I returned to Tokyo a few days later, I found Sensei pacing in her kitchen, sleepless for days despite drinking Kenneth's little beers at night and a concoction of teas and herbs from her daughter, the fortune teller.

Her clothes weren't wrinkled, her hair was combed. There were no raccoon circles under her eyes. She had dried her hair the night before in exactly the same way. It cleaved her neck icily above a simple blouse and cardigan. The room was spare as it always was, even on New Year's. Aside from the ritual narcissus from Sasaki-san, the antique dealer, there were no decorations of pine, no pyramid of clementines, no soft gooey rice cakes. There was not even the usual holiday bowl of *zoni*, broth.

She offered no new facts in the case, only repeated the moment of horror at the door. Like the music, there was no development, just repetition from a new angle, a relentless purging over and over again, especially the messy hair and boxer shorts, the push down the stairs, his feeble choice in women.

"He is weak. I can never forgive."

"He has a right to his own life," Judy said one night at a lesson.

"Oh really?" I said. "It's convenient now to be an ignorant gaijin, after all Sensei has done for him? This is fucking Japan, where nothing is free!"

From time to time I had pressed Sensei on this very point. Late in the evenings, after practice, while washing up at the kitchen sink, I would say, "Maybe some Japanese student might want to pay for your lessons." Even after Tomoko, I was unclear why she denied Japanese her lessons. To really revive this music she would need people who would stay, who could integrate it back into the culture. It was a matter of respect, I told her.

"They do not want to learn," she would say quietly. "They cannot enjoy music."

"Maybe you could teach them how," I said.

"I have to be formal, Janet. They will call me sensei. I am not a sensei. I am just a person."

"Of course, you're a sensei," I said, thinking, that she lacked the confidence to call herself one. I thought I knew her so well, thought that she needed me to save her, to point out all her fine qualities.

"In this society, I am nobody," she said, and turned to dry her hands. "But I am free."

≡

I refused to meet Kenneth to hear his side of the story. I did not return his phone calls or answer the apologetic letters that appeared in my mailbox. I did not want to be swayed into understanding. Steeling myself into rejecting him felt safer. He was exploiting Japanese culture, trampling its delicate beauty like Bigfoot. He was an imposter and a thief. Sensei calculated all she had paid over the years in lessons, recital fees, food, rent, over $20,000.

We had a recital planned for late January. "Can't we cancel?" I asked Sensei.

Her way of cutting him out was to invite him closer in. Even now, it was a conversation that could only be had in music. "Now is my revenge," she said. When he came for lessons, she set up the music table as usual, two shamisen head to foot across from each other, the pointy picks, the neat boxes of pencils in the middle. She sat across from him, demanding he teach her what she'd paid for him to learn on the flute. Tapping her foot, she hissed between breaths. "You are weak. Sensei hates you." He called himself her gigolo. "He is not human being!" she said. "Would it have been different if it was Janet?" he asked. I wondered about that, and what she would answer. There were so many holes in this drama but I dared not question a thing. The truth, I knew, for Sensei, was irrelevant. Like in our music, when translating a song, or looking at the old notations and trying to decipher what the old masters meant, she would tilt her head, "We can never know truth." The truth was impossible to find out. There was only the truth of the situation, and the situation was betrayal, it did not matter the details of what or how or why.

She went to his apartment and reclaimed every instrument she had given him, including her mother's shamisen—"Her poor spirit had to witness disgusting affair"—until only one bamboo flute remained. She related the tale of his betrayal to her flute teacher, who cut him off from any future lessons. She did the same with Kikuyu-sensei, who only seemed confirmed in her suspicions of haughty gai-jin. She said nothing to her own sensei, who would pass away on January 6, 1999.

In a matter of days, Kenneth had no more lessons, no more teachers, no way to practice Japanese music. Everything had been connected through Sensei. Years of introductions and lessons and good faith were snipped in a few visits.

The recital, Sensei said, would be his funeral.

=

I was jangled badly by what was happening. I was irritated every day, on pins and needles, like when the blood slowly dripped away from my feet as I played on my knees, leaving the whole top of the foot numb.

What if Sensei cut me out? What if I did something to offend, without knowing what it was? What if she interpreted some action of mine, something that seemed normal to me, as betrayal? She was responsible for more than my music: the shamisen stand, the phone, the fax, little things for the shamisen, notation, bridges, the new flecked oak pick. All those performances, all those relationships, were unquantifiable.

What really happened? Did I really have no thoughts of my own on the matter? Was undissolved fealty my only response? It was, I think, because it drove away the truer thought underneath that I envied Kenneth, because for all his unfaithfulness and lying, he was now free to go.

Cursing Kenneth calmed me down. The only option seemed to be to prove my loyalty, to stay close at hand, to agree.

To protect myself, I did nothing.

=

At the recital, Kenneth arrived pasty-faced with a cough. His singing voice was strained. I stood by Sensei, avoiding his balding head, his too-short kimono, his little lies and fatal flaws!

"He said he wanted to escape himself," Sensei said. "But he is too weak to commit to suicide."

After tuning the instruments and placing greeters at the door, we sat backstage waiting. The concert hour approached and passed. No guests arrived. We checked the concert program, the clocks, but everything was correct. One person wandered in. Soon we realized there had been some confusion with Kin-san, the futon seller, Kenneth's landlord, who was largely responsible for gathering the crowds for our events.

We all looked to Sensei, standing backstage holding her shamisen, for what to do. She nodded and led us on to the stage. We played every song straight through and then shifted off our knees, while our sole audience member applauded. It would have been better if no one had come.

Later, Sensei and I watched the video over a bowl of noodles in her rooms. There were no tiny cans of beer, no toasts, no candles. I don't know why we watched, except that we always wanted to hear the music and see how we'd come through. Halfway through the video, something caught our attention and we leaned in closer. The right corner of the screen was fogging up. The white cloud rose and approached the far edge of the stage where Kenneth sat, draining him of color and form until, finally, he vanished altogether.

=

Seiko called me once wanting to tell me her side of the story. She was sweet and apologetic, her halting English inadequate for such important things to say. She explained private matters I did not want to hear, how her husband was not affectionate, they had not slept together in eight years.

"Janeto-san, I am thirty-nine. This is my last chance to live as a woman."

I quit dance. Seiko had introduced me, and it was awkward now to see her at lessons. I talked this over with Sensei, and she taught me the long string of syllables I would need to say to beg to be released from her study. I couldn't just quit. Tachibana-sensei was saddened. She liked having a foreigner around to spice things up.

On the night Kenneth left Japan, I took Sensei to the theater. She preferred lately to watch not the overstated plots of the kabuki, but the cool remote beauty of the noh. The stories of restless souls coming back from the dead, the vigorous monk-like chanting, the Buddhist themes of suffering and salvation were a bracing change from gaudy illusion. It healed her.

In the spring of 1999, on the three-month anniversary of her teacher's death, Sensei took me to visit his widow. In Buddhist thought, ninety days after death is when the spirit crosses over into the afterlife. It is important to pray for their crossing so they don't get stuck between worlds.

I was uncomfortable around grief, even in my own culture. Sensei said we should offer to cook and clean for her teacher's widow. The ritual phrase to the grieving was similar to the one said after a meal, and I worried I would confuse them.

We made our way through the snowless streets of Hongo in the center of Tokyo. She pointed out along the way the grave of Uno Chiyo, a Japanese writer I was interested in. There were so many places unknown to me, so many streets where people lived, burrowed into their lives, the surfaces of which looked drab and uniform, but were not.

The widow met us at the door in a crumpled bathrobe. She started crying when she saw Sensei and soon collapsed on her small frame. We each took an arm and led her inside.

"What is to become of me?" she sobbed. Sensei talked in soothing tones.

The telephone rang constantly, most of the calls coming from one of Kikuoka-sensei's students, a geisha who kept asking him to come to the phone.

"She calls at all hours of the night," the widow said.

I'd never seen anything like this in Japan. Everyone was completely unstrung.

Since her teacher's death, Sensei had entered a period of consolidation, of re-organizing her life. She offered shamisen workshops to avoid one-on-one lessons. She wanted more time for her own playing. She took up dance again and invited me to join her.

For dinner, I took her to Volks, a steakhouse in the opposite direction of Gusto. She always seemed to find things to eat that I could not. Raw tuna at Gusto, and *natto*, fermented soybeans, at home. Here, it was slimy okra, which she liked for its healthy properties.

I started working at the magazine that carried Sensei's ad. I stood over the classifieds typists, making sure her ad appeared every week so she wouldn't have to keep faxing it.

At night we sat around the music table, with a candle and the green leather *nagauta* book, and worked on translations. *Urashima*, a Rip Van Winkle–tale of a fisherman who discovers Paradise beneath the sea but loses it when he opens a forbidden box. *Tatsumi Hakkei*, a portrait of the geisha quarter, with subtle tempos and low-slung vocals and a red-cheeked geisha waiting for her love.

She threw new pieces at me, hard pieces: *Sumidagawa*, "The Mad Woman of the Sumida River," in which a woman goes mad with grief over her dead son. *Toba no Koizuka*, "The Love Mound of Toba," in which a samurai mistakenly kills his lover instead of her husband. *Sankyoku Itonoshirabe*, which we called "The Lie Detector," in which a courtesan in the pleasure quarters is questioned about her lover's whereabouts and is forced to play three instruments to see if she is lying.

It was as if there were no time left and she needed to teach me as much as possible, or perhaps she needed to get something out of her. Maybe the songs reminded her of her teacher. I can't say. I didn't perfect these songs; we went through them deeply enough to learn their tricks and techniques, but they would never be performed.

I was aware now more than ever of the danger of Sensei's gifts, the duties they incurred. I should have been packing my bags, setting sail on a boat home, increasing the distance between us. Instead, while she cooked a simple evening meal, I ransacked her music, pulling out pieces I wanted to learn. My lessons had never been so productive, and yet I was still restless. When would it end?

At Sensei's teacher's house, the three of us went into a spare room, where an altar surrounded by chrysanthemums and lilies was set up. Sensei gestured for me to pay my respects. I knelt on the cushion and looked up at a portrait of her teacher smiling in his formal robes. Behind me the widow sobbed. Laundry was drying on racks around the room. Bins of clothing were piled everywhere. I had to think of something sad so I could cry. I owed that to Sensei, to show that I was affected, too, that her loss was my loss, though that day I knew I would never belong to her the way she belonged to this man. I knew then how far apart we were.

She did not belong to anyone now. She would make do with her teacher's lesson tapes in the bookcase, tapes that could warp in the sun or snag in the machine; would have to rely on his widow, now packing Sensei his shamisen, ivory picks, and his old cardigan; would have to depend on the memory of his soft *kakegoe*, literally "the hanging voice," cuing her silently as she played.

Her teacher's widow brought me coffee in a bone china cup, and while she and Sensei spoke in low tones in the kitchen, I sat on a chair in a Western sitting room, stirring in the cream with the tiny spoon, my back stiff against the hard cushions.

I protected Sensei even more after this, tending her, promoting her, conserving our bond. I stopped trying to innovate or change things.

She had won.

14

... cleansed of hesitation, stutters, and confusions ...

The one instrument I insisted on never playing was the flute. When I told Sensei no, she said okay and let me refuse. It was a surprise. Normally, I had to suffer through the endless pain and mistakes of a new music that I would never perform; it was humiliating.

Flutes were played, with rare exception, by Sensei's male students. Kenneth had specialized in flute, as did Alan. "So beautiful," she would say. "Like a dream." Kenneth tried to teach me once. "Imagine yourself blowing air over the top of a coke bottle," he said, puzzled that I could not make a sound in the tiny hole at the end of the bamboo tube. I handed it back to him, dizzy.

Without Kenneth, Sensei's flute sound got sweeter and more natural, almost human in its cry. She practiced before leaving for work in the mornings, on her lunch hour, before her students came at night. She never performed the flute. It seemed to be a kind of link between her and the men, or maybe a substitute for the men, some understanding I didn't share.

She ordered her flutes from an invalid in Nagoya, the brother of a coworker. The slim bamboo rolls came in different pitches; lower were fatter and longer, the higher were slimmer and shorter. The flute pitch had to match the pitch of the singer, often not known until rehearsal, or even arrival to the performance, and so professionals carried brocade silk sacks of every flute size to their gigs. They jostled and clicked against the outlier among them, the stout, dark noh flute that was double-rolled in cherry bark and bamboo to make its ghostly peal.

When Alan visited in August of 1999, Sensei insisted on a performance. "Explain this piece to Alan," she said at the music table, where we'd arrived almost immediately after Alan flew in to start practicing.

Miyako Furyu, written in 1947, was "Scenes of the Old Capital." The *furyu* of the title was misleading. This was a term that referred to Kyoto, and meant an aesthetic of refinement. Tokyo was never *furyu*, and Sensei and I had wondered, over many conversations at the little table, if the word was there to create nostalgia and call up a former Japan, when Kyoto was capital, for the song's debut would have been to the charred remains of the fire bombings, to MacArthur's Occupation headquarters at the Waco Building in Ginza, to a people rebuilding from defeat.

"Sound of many insects," Sensei added.

"Insects, how gross," Alan teased.

She laughed and handed him a new delight: a *mushibue*, a tiny double-barreled bamboo flute that looked like a cinnamon stick. Blowing it through a cup of shallow water made a cricket-like trill. Sensei was excited about the new toy; the tiny reed had cost twenty dollars.

I held the beat with the shamisen as they played. I knew the piece well, although I had not yet mastered its finale: the *yuki no aikata*, the snow solo, a whirling finale that imitated a snow storm.

The snow solo began with a single bass note, and then several, on the first string, gathering in slow eddies as the pick made its way steadily into a whirling blizzard of notes. One had to press carefully all the way through to the skin to try and keep the picking hand even. I got tangled again and again when I tried. It was why I had given up.

That the snow solo was hard was fair enough, but there was one note in particular that I took issue with. As if an affront to the musician who has made her way through the snare of dizzying picking and plucking, all sound stops and requires stillness: a single note. Its position is not unusual or rare, just a high six, a note often played and easily locatable. But in the tempo and trance one almost enters in trying to keep the strumming smooth, it is nearly impossible to find.

Every time I tried I was a beginner again, flailing on the neck, sending curdled notes into the air.

One day I found an old scratchy recording from the 1950s of the composer himself playing this piece. The composer was Kineya Jokan, who was Sensei's teacher's teacher's teacher. There was me–Sensei–Kikuoka-sensei–Yamada-sensei–Kineya Jokan. We were connected then.

I put the disc in and sat back and listened. There he was, making the shamisen sound like a child's toy, effortless and at ease. As he came out of the perfectly executed snow squalls, riding over his strings, his *bachi* in icy precision, he played the note, and to my surprise, the note that he played was flat. Was it a mistake? I replayed it. It wasn't too glaring but he was off. He did not hit a six. Not a perfect six anyway. Not a clean pure note.

I was confounded by this. Why would they record him if he hadn't gotten it right? Why not do another take until it was perfect? I wondered if he intended such a difficult solo so that we would have to work hard to master it, or to remind us that the learning never ends? Part of me wondered if he'd created an unplayable song. The piece ended with a final image of an umbrella under snow and then repeated. The musician could play the loop infinitely.

Alan's flute sounded a little reedy, but, as always, he was confident. As much as I chafed against the time the performance would take from our visiting together—we'd not seen each other in eight months—I was glad for the distraction. When Alan had arrived I felt distant. Sensei's words were in my ears. "You need your own life" and "Side by side," her two hands gesturing separate apartments.

Alan's letters enthralled me. They were beautiful missives, always handwritten, sometimes down to the nub of a pencil that broke off as he wrote, the way we used to fall asleep on the futon talking, heads at opposite ends.

But this was the problem. The letters weren't quite in this world. They offered up the best of us, they were a time apart, they were even more exciting than our talks on the phone, than speech in general. Cleansed of hesitation, stutters, and confusions, letters were not mundane or dross-filled humdrum lists. They were elevated. While still accounting for what we were doing and thinking, they always ended up going back to our origins, the Inland Sea, the stars that had collided that night, the benevolence of Japan itself.

I hinted to Alan that the distance wasn't good. That in staying apart we were missing something vital. I feared what was happening to him in my absence. Not other women, but experience, life, moments untranslatable. We had less a relationship than a hold on experience, *words*. With Sensei, I had few words, only experience.

Mostly I feared that we were creating something impossible to live up to, a life unlivable. "Soon," he said at every visit, promising to come back. "Soon."

=

It was hard to walk through Tokyo as a couple. We had to walk single-file to avoid cars in the narrow streets. Alan's six-foot, three-inch frame maneuvering around my six-foot-square room annoyed me. I walked daily through eighteen million people and was fine, but one person I loved in my room and I felt hemmed in.

That I felt this is no surprise. We were practically strangers again after eight months. But I took it as a kind of sign, that it must mean something, rather than talk to him about it. I could only feel annoyed at his size-thirteen shoes parked in the *genkan*, the wrappers from his favorite coconut sable cookies lining the trash, his big suitcase, his bags of souvenirs.

"It's like being in a movie, this place," he said at a Japanese pancake shop in Shibuya, spilling bonito flakes on the table. He didn't lean in and listen intently as I described a new drum pattern, and offered no *aizuchi*—connecting conversational murmurs of "uh-huh, uh-huh"—as the Japanese always did. He was staring off at a skyscraper, a tabi seller, the crowds pressing past. He didn't get my cues when I said "maybe" making a request, or "difficult" when I meant "no." He expected me to speak up. Unlike Sensei, who handed me a bottle of calamine lotion before I'd even noticed the itch, Alan couldn't anticipate my wishes or desires, and it all felt flattened, like the air was let out of something.

At the end of a noh play one night, we watched as the actor painstakingly left the stage, a process that took a good ten minutes as he minced glacially down the ramp, past the three pines, into the curtain that whooshed open at just the right moment, swallowing him up. It always made me weepy to witness the moment of leaving—of loss—stretched for as long as humanly possible.

"It's like they're dismantling the illusion along with the set in our presence," Alan said, fascinated.

Time, they took time. It was everything he and I didn't have—time—and to be without it was corroding, I warned. Time was the only comfort, the ultimate container. Time held you in place. Time allowed all kinds of things to get in, things you couldn't even remember anymore, things that slid through the skin and became natural reactions, like the trip of my heartbeat when I heard two wooden clogs knock against each other, or the sound of a singer's falsetto breaching over the slow tattoo of a shamisen.

In our not quite four years together, which Sensei later called our "golden time," I was acutely aware of time passing. There were many moments when I would look up from playing with Sensei, or a featured guest in her rooms, like the day we invited the shamisen inventor to come and sing because he never got to sing with live shamisen; or the handyman and his wife, who came with his son before the boy left for college in Germany, so he would know something traditional before he left. During these encounters I knew something important was passing, that my life, even, might never be better than this moment. I might even look back at it as my best years. I knew it wouldn't last, and that laced everything with bittersweetness. There were things here long before I was. They had weight and density and held me—an unbearable lightness—in their midst.

Without the weight of time, what did you have?

Something dreamy and interior faded inside in the presence of Alan as the language I understood too well filled my ears and the relationship unfurled without mystery. I was fluent in something else now, a language he didn't speak. We had fallen in love in the Inland Sea, out of time, and we hadn't landed yet.

=

Romeu, a bilingual Brazilian scientist, was emcee of our concert, held at a shrine, the very same of Kenneth's last appearance. Sensei called him "chairman." Pres, the Australian shakuhachi player was back, now studying at Sensei's alma mater with a shakuhachi master. A new student Caroline, a redhead from Cork, Ireland, sang *Kurokami*, the ballad "Black Hair," and made it sound less like the dirge I despised.

I paced the rooms as I always did before a performance, worried about fingerings, tuning slips, page-turning, *ma*. There were always new students to guide, students who were carefree, who would probably never do this again, for whom this was a lark. I chatted with them and moved on. I was wearing the summer kimono from Alan's show *Canton* two years before: creamy salmon with white cherry blossoms. My hair was now bobbed, shorter than Sensei's, and frizzed into spasms of curls from the humidity.

The last time we had performed at this shrine was January, with Kenneth. It was now summer, with the sun blazing and lots of people coming. As I paced around idly, I decided to peek out at the stage and the large tatami space for the audience. Sensei and Alan were leaning against the proscenium, warming up their flutes.

She was wearing the black formal robe with cranes stitched at the hem and my favorite kimono coat: a sophisticated purple and white dyed *yabane* arrow pattern. Alan's tone was softening as he followed Sensei's fingerings, from breathy wisps to a thin honeyed stream. The sleeves of his kimono came to his forearms and the hem to his calves. During *Canton*, it was funny, like when he wore the Rising Sun headband and trick glasses at rehearsals and made crazy *kakegoe* as he played the drums. That impulse, I think now, might have been to cover for the humiliations of how we learned—through negative correction—and allowed him to go on, for I knew he felt awkward. It also made Sensei laugh and cheered her up from her endless ringing pleas of unfairness, of greed, of the difficulty of the Japanese.

In other words, he had a whole way of relating to Sensei that I didn't know about but would have to navigate should the three of us continue on like this. How to communicate mine?

So much had seeped in beyond Sensei's music. I had absorbed her way of hanging towels on the laundry hangers, two corners on one clip; her way of making tea, eyeballing the leaves to the size of a ¥10 coin; the way I dropped my slippers when going from room to room, the fact that I even wore slippers; her way of shopping, carrying bags in the crook of her elbow, hands folded together, standing at a diagonal and peering at goods, head tilted. I used phone cards that had pretty Edo images; bought pink pickled radish and her favorite seaweed from the cutting floor at New Year's; imitated the unique way she held her chopsticks, guided by the middle finger not the index. I stored incense sachets with my kimono, tucked a tiny fan in my obi or a handkerchief when eating to serve as a bib. I tied on a kimono to practice when feeling tired, as she did, letting the obi's tension energize me.

I leaned into her rhythms, her notes over mine like a mother's hand guiding a child to spell her name. The faint echo of her toe tapping the beats to steady me, her chuckling at my mistakes, our wondering who messed up worse, her telling me we needed a "trick" when arriving at a difficult passage. There were quiet moments when I became cranky at a mistake, and had to stop and pencil in her notes. But I'd then follow the excited turn of the page to the next vertical column of numbers, waiting to hear where her voice would dart and swerve, how the shamisen would shape it, how the two would form a whole.

My neck flushed, my stomach twisted. They suddenly were simply too far away to reach. The stage, the floor cushions, and concert programs became a chasm impossible to cross.

=

I rode the trains to the airport with Alan a week later, out past the rice fields, where the city ebbed and the rocks and sea appeared. I waved as he went through security and collected his bags, and kept waving until he turned the corner and was lost in the crowd. I didn't want him gone, but I wanted the pain of him gone.

Instead of going home, I changed trains at Tokyo Station and headed to Ginza. The train car was half empty. I saw my face in the glass in the tunnels, and listened to the conductor's polite murmur. At Ginza I transferred to the Hibiya Line, silver on the maps, the business district. I got off at Higashi-Ginza and climbed out of the tunnel, looking for the great wing of roof tiles of the Kabuki-za. I cut around the side for a one-curtain ticket and climbed to the balcony. The stage was black. A flute sounded and the lights shifted to deep indigo. A low moan escaped the singer's lips, a lone shamisen plinked. When lights came up, paper confetti snow covered the stage, falling onto the white paper umbrella, white kimono, and white hood of the Heron Maiden, like a bride inching her way across the stage.

I tumbled into the dance, the fury and anguish of the bird, beating its bloodied wings before taking her last breath. The actor was Tamasaburo, the best female impersonator of our times. Tama-chan, Sensei called him. Do we diminish the things we love? All I remembered of that dance, and Alan's visit, was the dancer's tabi during her first few steps onto the stage, fresh, new, clean, sliding out from under the hem, a tiny hoof, about to reveal itself.

15

... utterly her own creation ...

A shamisen lesson is tense. There are too many holes to fall into, silent spaces to violate, ways to humiliate yourself. The rest of that summer, something in me went limp. I made mistakes on the shamisen. Several of them. I coughed, I apologized, I made excuses. The notes came, dormant and sluggish. And the thought came, too, that maybe, to Sensei, I was just another temporary white face in a kimono holding a shamisen. This feeling made me itchy and uncertain. I feared I was wasting time, and this would all add up to nothing.

As we approached recital season that fall, the next song in my repertoire was *Gekizaru*, a lively "Monkey Dance." Kikuyu-sensei, our drum teacher, wanted Sensei and me to perform it for her drum students at her annual drum recital at Halloween. There would be only three of us: me, a professional lead, and Sensei, who would play the capo line one octave higher, in tight-clipped counterpoint.

I decided to memorize the piece.

"Don't waste brain space, Janet," Sensei said. "No meaning."

Memorizing took away from her teaching duties. She had students to train, shamisen to find them, and tabi and kimono, so many details. "I will disappoint Kikuyu-sensei," she said, and sighed, turning to her notation.

Sensei never asked me to memorize a piece. But for me, it was the true mark of a professional. I wanted to know if I could do it.

Sensei was irritable as we practiced. She played the main line with me so I could practice the memorization, taking time away from her capo practice.

As we played, she stopped me. "Wait!"

I double-backed and tried to match her timing.

"Still too soon. You have to move at the proper time."

But wasn't racing to the next note to play it in tune preferable than playing it out of tune?

She shook her head. Visual unity was part of the music's beauty. Everyone had to be in synch.

She showed me a tip. "You can check," she said, and I watched as she arrived at the note at the last minute, and then, with just a flick of her fingertip, tested the string to make sure it was the right note before sounding it with her pick.

"This is cheating," she said. Cheating was okay, but, like every other rule and form, it had to be done in exactly same way.

I practiced the "Monkey Dance" diligently in my room, attempting a smooth and quick transition in each of the five tuning changes. But even if I leapt quickly, I often fell flat or sharp and had to find another space quickly to retune. Again, I was learning that the notes were the least of it on the shamisen. First there was the learning of critical spaces, *ma*. Now I wrestled with keeping the instrument in tune, another of its challenges to be mastered.

As for notes, moving at the last second as Sensei instructed was hopeless. I had to stop the tape and tune up or find the note before moving on, a luxury I would not have on stage. Still, I began to consider the performance a kind of graduation.

I wanted to improve, for her as much as me. I wanted to impress her. It was for her that I practiced this monkey romp. For her that I worked on tuning quickly and cleanly, that I even took on the challenge of tuning at all. I didn't think how any of it would look or appear to others. I was hoping for a perfect performance. I needed one to quell the unease about where she was leading me. I needed to be undeniable. I couldn't afford a mistake.

I took on difficult drum pieces and insisted on memorizing them, too: the hand-drum duet in *Urashima*, the Rip Van Winkle tale, and *Hanami Odori,* "The Blossom Viewing Dance," which included lurching conversations with the companion lap drum. Kikuyu-sensei was tickled by my arrogance.

"The Blossom Viewing Dance" was one of the most difficult drum pieces in the repertoire, not only for its endless strands of poms and pops, requiring sheer force and strength. Its difficulty boiled down to what was the difficulty everywhere in Japan: entering. Once you were in the pattern, you were safe. But it was the launch of the pattern that vexed. The year before, it was what had led Kihiro-sensei into a whole different song during our drum recital.

Despite how it would appear, what I wanted with Sensei—what I needed—was a way to stay close to her, to be on stage side by side dissolving into sound, as before. Since her teacher died, since Kenneth left, since my ambivalence about Alan's return grew, I had begun to turn to things outside her rooms. I took acting classes and studied haiku with a poet in the neighborhood. I went to puppet plays and read Japanese writers. I traveled to Okinawa and played the small snake-covered *jabisen,* and to Nagano to bathe in its hot springs.

I hadn't ever had time and money to explore like this before. Alan said it was like I was writing my own cultural grant. I knew that much of it had to do with Sensei and her music, watching her pursue a passion, carve a life out of what she loved.

When I began working at the magazine where Sensei ran her ad, I chose to interview a longtime expatriate who had been in Tokyo since the Occupation. I met him at the Press Club in Yurakucho and we talked over a meal, high above the Ginza, not far from the American postwar headquarters. Honestly, I still had difficulty with the image of a people grateful for defeat. Were they really? Why?

The conversation didn't go there, though. We talked about his long life in Tokyo, what he'd seen, what had changed. Once, in the 1950s, he'd seen a wall being built around a great tree so as not to cut down the tree. "That would never happen now," he said.

He didn't protest the changes, though. He looked forward to them, in fact. He was so much more sophisticated than me. He could see the Japanese clearly, watch their arts become taxidermy, see them rush to Western values, and not love them any less. It was like every-thing was as it should be. It was hard to understand. Most difficult was when he talked about himself.

Being in Tokyo was like being a fish out of water, he said, but he liked the perspective of the outsider. He cultivated it. The only thing to remember about living here, he said, was to not try to fit in.

It seemed the loneliest thing in the world to me, to be out on the margins, an outsider. I nodded and wrote it down in my notebook.

I remember another thing he told me that I didn't understand for a long time, but I think I do now. He said the best observers of Japan were the people who stayed less than six weeks or longer than ten years. For neither is there the push-pull need to go away and come back, be consumed and repel. For neither is there the need to see themselves through the eyes of the Japanese. For neither is ambivalence a factor.

I wanted Sensei's blessing for all my new interests, but I did not know how to get it except for music. When my acting teacher called to tell me, "You're really good, you could do something with this. Study with me," I refused and ran to a shamisen lesson. I had to do something in Sensei's world, something that would stun her all over again and make her want to enfold me in her universe forever.

I also wanted to surpass her, unequivocally, in plain sight. From what followed these events, I can say, too, that it seems that on another level, deep and festering, something in me was itching for a fight. To blow everything up and shatter it.

=

I was irritated then when Sensei invited me to meet a new stu-dent one September evening. There was much to practice. Lucky Seven Boulevard was dusky, the air slightly crisp.

When I arrived Sensei and Sasaki-san were hovering over a vin-tage shamisen recently arrived in his shop, marveling at the carvings inside the sound box below a torn skin.

With them was Gautam, whom she had summed up on the

phone in her usual "shami-psychology" as a genius. He was a prodigy on the Indian stringed instrument, the veena, and a mathematical wizard.

She suggested we make small talk while she work out the particulars with Sasaki-san.

"Janet is my longest student," she told him. "Please ask her about shamisen."

She had given him the text of *Urashima*, which we had translated after Kenneth's abrupt departure.

"This is beautiful!" he said. "Are you a poet?"

Gautam had written a whole book of poetry to a cousin, whom he was in love with and wanted to marry, but it had not worked out.

While Sasaki-san's hair smoothed into inky stillness, Gautam's wriggled into curls. Sasaki-san mumbled, Gautam blurted. Sasaki-san's cheeks blushed, Gautam's were pressed into smiles and giggles. I started to feel like we were school children acting out in class while the teachers talked.

After Sasaki-san left, Sensei set down a tray of hot *sobacha* on the floor between us where we sat on green silk cushions. "Guess where we are going this weekend?" she said to me and looked at Gautam.

He half-bowed to Sensei from his cushion. "Please be my guests at my house. I will cook. You don't need anything except the instruments."

"People, instruments, all just sleep together!" Sensei said and made with her lips the round "O."

=

Gautam treated Sensei like a queen. When he met us with friends at his station in Adachi Ward in northeast Tokyo the next Saturday morning, he asked her if she was tired from the hour-long ride and ordered cabs to deliver her and her half-dozen students to his apartment. A festival was winding through the streets in front of the station, its portable shrine teetering on the shoulders of grunting men in loincloths.

I joined Sensei in a cab with Gautam's friend Nachi, who wore a long shirt to his knees over pajama-like pants of cool white linen that set off his coffee-colored skin. His eyes were like heavy-lidded black pools that looked out sleepily from behind his glasses as he talked about a pair of camphor lions he had recently acquired in Hong Kong. Sensei was intrigued. She was wearing the purple arrow kimono coat over a simple kimono.

A man with a sunny disposition met us at the door. A breeze was coming in from the open veranda. Sensei looked around the place and followed when Gautam pointed to his music room. She peered inside. "So gorgeous," she said. Unlike her shelves stuffed with scores and tapes and concert programs, where she was never able to find anything, this room contained only the sweetly scented straw mats, a low table with a candle, and, at one end, behind floor cushions, a long instrument with a fat fretted neck and what looked like a gourd at one end.

Sensei was quite social, fluttering around the room, graciously receiving the plate of curry and naan she was handed by Gautam, who had cooked. He was in a gold shirt and chinos. "Nice taste," she said to me.

"Isn't it too hot?" I knew she didn't like spices. But she ignored my comment and instead tore the oily bread with her hands.

She hadn't taken off the coat inside, which I found strange, and said so. She just shrugged.

After lunch, we went into the music room where Gautam climbed onto the cushions behind the veena. Seven fat tuning pegs controlled the strings: four for melody, three for rhythm, he explained. After turning on a small amplifier, his fingers began to flutter over the strings in rock-like arabesques. Nachi thumped on a tabla drum and called out something we couldn't understand. Gautam strummed and called out something else. Nachi passed the drum to one of Sensei's students and began to sing, bleating notes in a rhythmic pulse.

As Gautam played, his little finger coaxed a drone while he finger-picked above, producing a rich celestial sound. Sensei listened, eyes down, hands in her lap.

Indian music was composed of ragas, scales that recombined in endless patterns, not unlike mathematics, Gautam said, his dark eyes darting around the room, wriggling on his cushion.

After a few questions from the students, Gautam half-bowed from his cushion. "Sensei? What do you think? How about a duet?"

Cheers went up in the room for the dueling banjos.

She did not correct him when he called her Sensei.

"What should I play?" she asked me. She was flustered, I could tell.

"Anything. Just improvise," I said.

"Not so easy," she said and looked down at the *yubikake* she slid onto her thumb and index finger. It was tan and of a thicker weave than ours. She had crocheted it herself; I had seen the tiny needles resting on the hutch one day during a lesson.

"Take a riff from some song," I said. I threw out names of difficult pieces.

"*Miyako Furyu,*" I dared her.

She struck a low tattoo on the bass string and I recognized the hushed world of falling snow. Of course. She had chosen the snow solo. Everything else was a duet.

Gautam closed his eyes as Sensei's notes gathered in slow spirals and then whirled into a blizzard of notes. Gautam imitated them several beats behind, as in a round. On they went, splitting, slicing, shaving the air with razors of sound. Sensei advanced in icy precision, her tiny form compact on the floor, steady and stable, her hair in a precise line at her neck.

Sensei didn't like risk. She chose to play it safe on the stage with her students and her concerts. But now, when she came to the end of the solo, she looped back and played it again. Gautam tried to keep up, his fingers popping and plucking new shapes. She looped again. She seemed to refuse to end. A third time, a fourth. Finally she stopped short and reached for the impossible note. It was closer than I'd ever heard it.

I watched her tiny folded form, the purple arrow *haori* jacket of a chic geisha. I had only rarely seen such steeliness in her and that was at the beheadings after a concert. "Tomorrow is new life." She never looked back. When Kenneth left her, she did the same thing. So much ambiguity, confusion, and waiting, and then the moment for utter decision.

I saw now that she had in her anything she wanted. Masterful skill, despite not becoming a professional. Her foreign students. Her lessons. Her trips to Kyoto. Her drums. Her shamisen. She had everything she needed. She lost her mother and Kenneth, and she lost her teacher, but she would make do with her lesson tapes and his recordings, with the memory of his soft voice cuing her as she played.

She did not belong to anyone now. She was alone and she would survive, and I knew that I would not.

=

Sensei released a confidence at Gautam's that I had never seen before. She never showed it, or claimed it for herself even. But I could now see that she had it. Everyone could see, and it was dazzling, this display of her skill, her ability to go on and on. I seemed to dissolve from the room as I listened, like a melting piece of the snow she was thrashing with her pick. What could I ever be master of in Japan? I would always be scrambling after her the way Gautam was now on the veena.

Toward evening, people started to leave. Sensei was one of the first to go, as usual. She retired early, and kept to her routines. At the door, she paused, and looked back and asked if I was okay staying. How would I get back?

Gautam said he'd see that I got a cab back to the station.

I watched her mince to the elevator, hands folded, a few students trailing with her bags. One by one, the other students left, until the final one, a British violinist asked if I wanted to share a cab to the station.

"There's more curry! We can go on all night!" Gautam laughed.

I stayed because there was something I wanted to do. I returned to the music room, now lit with candles. Someone poured wine.

Gautam's fingers fluttered, his friend Nachi chanted. They listened to each other and responded, in a kind of trading fours. They asked me to join on the shamisen. While one played, the others released sighs, moans, sucking sounds with their tongue, as if taking the music in physically.

The shamisen could not compete with the veena, amplified and powerful. My silk strings sounded soft and timid. I plucked harder.

When Sensei wanted a student to stay, she never directly asked or revealed her hope that they might. It was always in terms of a seduction, of her luring you with some moment of beauty, some not-to-be-missed opportunity, some promise of sweet reward. "You should stay in Japan," she would say, eyes shining, looking directly at you. Or if she really wanted to play—Sensei loved games—she would tilt her head and let her voice rise into a singsong plea, as if to see how long she could keep the charade going, for the student and, perhaps, for herself, until she would burst out laughing, "No, it's up to you."

I felt sometimes that with me, she had not yet gotten to the punch line, the moment when she would burst forth, open-mouthed, and declare the game was over.

=

Gautam was always moved by something: a cloud, a mathematical equation, the dancing figures in a ballet studio over the station. He wrote a poem comparing me to the note 4#. He wrote reams of poems, sometimes scribbling them in the endnotes of paperbacks.

When I returned to Gautam's the next weekend alone, I brought my shamisen and a sheaf of haiku. "These are wonderful! So lovely! Listen to this, …" and he read aloud to Giri, another musical friend.

We listened to Giri sing ragas, which told stories. For lunch Gautam made us broccoli sandwiches.

"How long have you been studying with Sensei?" Gautam asked, setting out the platter of food and crossing his legs.

"This month is my three-year anniversary."

Gautam sucked his tongue and looked, open-mouthed, to Giri. Giri hugged his elbows and smiled. "Wonderful."

"You are brilliant, my dear. And all those silences, what is it called, *ma*? And Sensei, what a wonderful teacher she is!" He spiraled his hand into the air. Everything to Gautam and Giri was wonderful, beautiful, and mysterious. They made it seem like life could be one big veena dream, a continuous party of music and little else.

I went back to Gautam's often, arriving alone at the outlying station. Suburban Tokyo had always depressed me, with its knock-off department stores and smoky pachinko parlors. The False City, Alan and I called these outposts. Now the suburbs were pleasantly anonymous as I got into one of a long line of yellow taxis, gave the driver Gautam's address, and sat back and lit a cigarette. The only sounds were the radio of the dispatcher, the whisper of the driver's white gloves on the wheel. I got out at the large apartment complex and rang the bell. When I entered the spacious rooms I felt relief.

The highlight was the music. One of us played a phrase while Gautam's friends Giri and Nachi, who were usually there, listened with bowed heads. When finished, the next person took up the strand, continuing it in a new way. I worried that my riffs were not interesting enough, that they were simple and childish. I took a drag on someone's cigarette in the ashtray, squinted through the smoke. My head was full of wine, my fingers clumsy. I worried about getting the shamisen neck sticky. I licked wine off my fingers while Gautam watched me with his dark eyes.

I tried to find some scrap of music in my head, some note that had reached me, to expand and transform into something of my own. To improvise. They all sounded tinny, the shamisen impotent. Not because I could not play but because I could not get out of the form. Every time I tried, I ended up in one of Sensei's songs. I was where I'd left off with piano. I had never understood music's creation. I had only played songs others composed.

I turned to the ragas. Their intervals were more unbalanced than Japanese music, less of a commitment to melancholy than a constant fluttering from joy to pain, ecstasy to sorrow in scales that embraced both or couldn't decide on either.

Gautam took shamisen lessons from Sensei, and even Nachi and Giri signed on. She knew that I was going to his house to play music. She thought it was too far. I should save my time.

The transition to more than friends was quick and fevered. Gautam respected my relationship to Alan. I insisted we were just friends, he lived so far away.

=

A few weeks later, I sought Sensei out at Gusto to share with her my secret: I was in love with Gautam. The leaves had not yet fallen on Lucky Seven Boulevard and the night was warm. Traffic was busy. At five o'clock it was already dark.

Sensei was sitting with Kathleen, a new Australian student. I sat down with them and ordered a coffee and black tea cake. Sensei was trying to get Kathleen on a regular lesson schedule. Her first must have gone well if their lesson had strayed into dinner. Sensei only did that when she was comfortable. I nodded, adding bits about the kabuki, concerts, the tricks of the instrument. The dinner was an informal business meeting. I was always trying to sell Sensei. "Gaijin has a power," she said.

On the subject of Gautam, I said this: he was not a snob, he had musical talent, and really appreciated me. The words could have been Sensei's, and they had the effect I was looking for.

"Wow," she said. "You can be happy in Japan."

We left the restaurant and began to make our way back to Sensei's rooms. It was just around the corner, but she walked slowly and seemed to be thinking of something. The air was charged with purpose and excitement, as it always was around her. She began ruminating again about all the possibilities for music, about everything we could do.

Dividing us from the road was the low hedge and steel railing. Four lanes of traffic cruised past, the small cars of Tokyo with right-side drivers. Above were green highway signs filled with square squiggles and Roman letters. Kathleen stood smiling and eager.

Sensei stood smiling, too, her dark hair shiny under the street lamps, her music tote on her arm as usual, hands clasped.

"Now you can stay in Japan longer," she said, beaming and just for that moment under the yellow lamps, with Tokyo rushing past us on Lucky Seven Boulevard, everything was perfect.

By perfect, by now it should be clear, that I meant, dead.

=

On October 31, we arrived at the seaside hotel in Kamakura in late morning for our concert with Kikuyu-sensei. Gautam had greeted Jane, Sensei, and me in Shibuya with a tray of Starbucks coffees. On the train, Sensei was quiet. I watched the amber and golden leaves out the window and listened to Jane and Gautam talking softly. My heart was pounding. I felt Sensei's disappointment and disapproval.

She had begun to question my decision. "Strange, you have very good *ma*, sense of timing, you can wait in the music. In life, very different." It was too fast, was I sure? What about Alan, wasn't he coming someday, we'd live in apartments side by side and study with her and put on concerts and be a family again? I ignored her searching eyes and soft inquiries. I was making decisions now. I called Alan. It was over, I told him, we were just friends. At Gautam's I chewed betel nut, my head reeling from the nicotine.

At Sensei's lessons, I came in the door as usual, dropped my music bundle and shoes with large gestures, as if to approximate normalcy. It was the same apartment, the same neighbors; another autumn in Tokyo with a recital to prepare and new students to train. Sensei was waiting as usual with tea and a light supper, some music on the table planned for the afternoon or evening. She said little and I began to enjoy this quality of the Japanese that had always frustrated me –the need to say little—polite taciturn people who kept the most important things private and unexplained.

"Are you sure?" she asked, looking at me as if squinting into the sun.

"Yes," I said and turned, with sudden fascination, to a new bridge or pick.

It was the same music room. In the morning, it was still flooded with sunlight coming through the lace curtains. In the evening, with the doors latched, it was stark under the fluorescent lamps.

"Do you trust me?" she asked one evening.

I dismissed the question—what did trust have to do with anything?—and began to race through the next solo, pushing her to a faster speed. I wanted the music to match my life, which was now going very fast.

Since the affair started there was no more slow release of ancient secrets, no waiting or holding back. Now there was speed in the form of taxi cabs rushing us to expensive dinners and pricey nightclubs. In the back seat, I rolled my tongue in Gautam's mouth, one eye on the rearview mirror, wanting the prim white-gloved driver to see.

In restaurants, we spilled drinks, filled the ashtrays. He kissed me deeply at the table until the Japanese waiters were too embarrassed to approach. I was out all the time, looking in on a world I now felt I had been missing out on. I no longer looked wistfully at the young beautiful crowds of Shibuya and Aoyama but saw them now as a backdrop for my own breeze and wit.

We didn't walk we dashed—into nightclubs, taxis, ATMs. We didn't read Krishnamurti, we gulped him down. We didn't sip drinks but slurped them, watching each other while licking the rim. I no longer wanted to buy the latest Japanese conversation books, which I often took home and studied faithfully. Instead we bought armloads of poetry books and tapes, more Krishnamurti.

Now, as we rode to the recital on the train, I watched the balconies of the apartment buildings of Tokyo. They were not verandas of pleasure with barbecue grills and lawn chairs like in America, but practical places for washing machines, clotheslines, and futons soaking up the sun. They were spaces of work, of the daily struggle to keep things organized and clean. Sensei hung her laundry out nearly every day. She beat her futon with a bamboo paddle and clipped it to air out every weekend. Sidewalks were rinsed by shopkeepers to keep the dust down. Crisp paper wrapped every purchase no matter how banal. No one put packages on the ground or the floor of the train. Wet hand towels—chilled in summer, scalding in winter—were served before a meal. No shoes were worn in the house.

But clean was not only about germs and dirt. Clean was a state of mind. Clean was the stone pool at the entrance of a Shinto shrine or a bowl of smoke at a Buddhist temple to purify your spirit. It was cleaning Tachibana-sensei's dance studio in the time-consuming old-fashioned way: on our feet pushing rags with our hands. It was the purity of Sensei's mission, her monk-like devotion to the music, her celibate celebration of passion.

Cleaning was about maintenance, the way so many things were in Japan; the instruments that needed constant care in the changing seasons; the human relationships that were held in place like the constellations with seasonal gifts. Sensei's apartment, worn but immaculate, maybe more immaculate because it was so worn.

There was nowhere that dirt accumulated more readily than on the soles of tabi. The herringbone pattern had to be scrubbed by hand after every wearing. I tried just throwing them in the washer and it never worked. I often just bought a new pair instead. I see now that the slight fraying of Sensei's tabi was not poverty or because she didn't want to wear a new pair. An old pair was more valuable. Her having taken care of it made it dearer. She herself gave it a value far beyond money.

Perhaps she had worn those tabi that day, and many times after, to remember herself amid the frittering rituals that made her feel alone and foreign in her own land. What she had was something that could never be bought. It was utterly her own creation.

I was unclean now, something in me ruined, and I reveled in Sensei seeing me this way. This is me, I said to her silently. This is me. This is me. This is me.

=

When we arrived I looked around the hall for Kikuyu-sensei. She came out from a group of women to welcome us with her usual raspy *Irrasshai!*, cigarette in hand, girlish head tilting, but then someone came with a question and took her away. I saw Kihiro-sensei but she didn't seem to remember me, or want to talk. Sensei, as usual, quietly attended to her instruments, keeping busy probably to avoid interactions. The pro we would play with I didn't know, but I nodded her way, and she smiled graciously but fakely, I thought. In the ladies' room I tried to make a joke about kimono but didn't get much of a response, only, "Isn't it too tight for you?"

When performing with Sensei, no matter where she was on stage, I knew she was there. Somewhere in the drums, or the shamisen, her tiny figure packaged in her kimono so tidily, her small hands and fingertips, like hammers, with tiny callouses, arriving in perfect timing to perfect notes. Backstage was always a reminder of the places I could never go with her, but onstage we were always striving together.

Now a foreignness had emerged. The feeling persisted onto the stage. Her notes came up to me on my left, tense and pinched, darting between the notes of the professional player on my right, who was staring at the walls while her fingers performed feats of magic.

I felt alone on the stage, like I used to feel at my piano recitals, approaching the bench stiffly, then turning and bowing—when did I bow in daily life? only at church—and sitting down on the cold hard bench—also church—the voices would begin, *Who do you think you are? You can't do this!* By the end, I was exhausted and defeated, no matter how well I did.

It was deep into the third tuning of the "Monkey Dance," when I'd lost myself and was sailing away free, that I heard the crack. It amplified and became the only sound in the room; the plinking of Sensei's capo went underwater. A hotness rose up from my neck. The audience blurred.

The tuning peg of my second string unspooled. The string slackened but did not break. If it had, I would have been handed a spare shamisen by a stage hand. I laid the shamisen out on the floor in front of me, working quickly. I brought the tuning peg to my hip bone, pressed in and turned, coiling the string, testing its firmness, and then brought it back to my lap to continue. I was able to finish the piece.

Thinking now, it seems a marvel, a true test of what I knew and could do at the time, not unlike in the Junior Miss contest of my youth, when I had forgotten the whole middle of the "Minute Waltz" and sailed home on my own inventions.

Part of the skill of a shamisen player is to reckon with the disturbing fact that nothing was holding it in tune except you. That as you played, it was going to immediately start changing its sound, and your ears had to detect it, your hands correct it. Skill is becoming part of the instrument itself, ears pricked for pitch.

Success was losing yourself, not finding yourself.

I left the stage quickly after *Gekizaru*, feeling like a fool, convinced this was now quite public evidence that I definitely did not have what it takes. Sensei had been wrong, I had been wrong. It is remarkable, I think now, the lengths we will go to stay in a pattern, an endless loop, even if that pattern is our demise. It makes me think of Alan's talk of the salmon swimming upstream, the human impulse to follow the current to its final destiny.

But a shamisen is just a tool, an instrument, a chance to make something. It is not a destiny at all. Sensei herself would tell me years later. "It was never about music. Of course, it is about special people."

Sensei found me in the green room. "So bad shamisen tuning," she said.

I brushed it off. "Well, out of my control … " and walked to the beach and drank iced coffee in the sea breeze with Gautam.

"It could happen anytime, anywhere," I said. "You see, that's why the shamisen is so tricky … "

16

... the great leap out into the world ...

No single factor shaped my leaving Japan more than Sensei herself, just as a few years before, no single factor had more shaped my staying. I can still see that day clearly in my mind, of meeting her at the train station, the bright green telephone receiver in her hand, held away from her shining cape of hair, the tiny wooden sandals, the cool blueness of her robe, and my white blouse wilting in the heat.

Three weeks after my affair with Gautam began, we were standing in her kitchen, after a lesson. Those three weeks had been a lifetime. I had performed, traveled to Malaysia to visit my brother, there on business, had paddled up into the rain forest, had come home again and spun around town with Gautam in a kind of manic energy. It was now mid-November, 1999, three years and two months after first meeting Sensei. The crisp golden fans of the ginkgos on the big road were fluttering again and falling to the sidewalk.

The fluorescent lamps haloed us in her tiny kitchen. She served tea, and the cup was too hot to sip from, and so I stood holding it on its coaster, uselessly, while she paced. We had just played a lesson without saying anything. I don't think we even looked at each other.

She seemed to be thinking hard about something. Finally, she squinted up at me and said, "Are you sure, Janet? About Gautam? What about Alan?"

"What do you mean?" testing the cup again.

"Even if he suicides?"

"What are you talking about? He wouldn't do that."

She put down her teacup. "Janet, I am going to U.S."

"When? Why?"

"I will go to Chicago to teach shamisen to Alan's students."

"Are you coming back?"

I had lost her, I thought. It has finally happened.

"Just one week," she said, turning to wash her hands.

And then I had her again. It was just a moment, but that was it. I woke up, as from a sleep. Or rather it was the first jolt of an awakening that would come full circle a few days later in my room. At my first shamisen lesson I had seen what was possible for my life on the shamisen, in Japan. Now I was seeing what I could lose.

It would later bother Alan that I had come back to him because of a fear of losing Sensei. "Was it true?" he wanted to know. Would I have come back to him if Sensei were lost to me?

If I lost Sensei, my own life would lose importance, vigor, its very purpose, and it would be a kind of death. I would not exist in a way I wanted to anymore. And without that, there would be no Alan, no future.

Once, an old family friend tried to trick me. "Who do you love more, your mother or your father?" Because there was a question, I assumed there had to be an answer. I was raised to answer the question. I was not raised to question the question, to believe the question itself might ever be wrong.

I had chosen my mother. Mother was safety, my origin, the beginning of it all. Mother was the place you ran *from*. But father, I should have told him, father was the place you ran *to*, and running to father was the great leap out into the world.

=

People rarely leave Japan intact. It unravels them, stirs things up inside, and if there is no way to organize it, to figure it all out, it can rattle like old bones for the rest of your days.

I ran home from Sensei's room that night. "Go," she said, relieved that I had returned to my senses. "He is waiting."

I dialed Alan's number, calculating the time change, hoping he would answer.

It was easier to repair my relationship with Sensei. The Japanese didn't need details. They are concerned with the long view, a philosophical one, the essence as it applied to universal experience.

But with Alan, details were exactly what he needed. Where had I been? What was I thinking? I answered with surgical precision, a light cast now in my mind where for three weeks there had been narrow shadows. But to the question he asked most, returning to it over and over again, I had no answer. "What did you tell yourself to make this okay?"

I hadn't. I wasn't thinking anything, I told him. But then the question came back. There had to be some thought, some way to make it doable, this act of betrayal. But nothing came. It was like facing those drums scores at the beginning and not knowing a thing and feeling angry about it, almost violent, like if I didn't figure it out I'd kill someone.

But while facing these questions, more than any one answer, it was the fact that we kept talking that slowly helped me realize that I was as responsible for the vast distances between us as much as anyone was. I always held part of myself back, in music and in life, a sliver no one could touch, a part I couldn't share.

I coiled the phone cord around my fingers tightly as we talked, as if loosening my grip would lead him to change his mind, decide, after all, that my flaws were too great.

I called Gautam to tell him I was going back to Alan.

"I'm sorry, but I was confused. I want to work it out."

Who was the girl slurping drinks and licking wine off his fingers? It was part of me, too, I could now see clearly, a part that could sever as icily as Sensei's beheadings.

Gautam was irritated. "Love is not shopping," he said, offering a final lesson from Krishnamurti. "You can't just use people like Kleenex and throw them away."

"Don't spend your love on someone who doesn't value it, I guess is the lesson. I'm sorry, Gautam. Goodbye."

Thoughts of Alan filled the room. The Inland Sea, its subtle passageways, tiny islands, the waves gently lapping at the shore. The salt before the baths, when we scrubbed and scrubbed and dipped in and heated to fatigue. The crinkled map, with the yellow highlighter marking passage, eight hundred miles, from Tokyo to Hiroshima, the circle around Miyajima, the leap onto Shikoku, crossing over to the mainland, hugging the shore back up to Tokyo.

Alan loved me despite my inability to love him back.

Sensei herself had said of love, "I don't want to lose control." She chose her life for her own reasons. Music was honorable, she said. Love was selfish, a weakness, a loss of control. It had no place in Japan, this kind of intimacy: messy, full of mistakes, without edges or borders, unclear and untidy. Sensei dealt with this by imposing order on it. The shamisen itself had become a container for sadness and yearning, impossible loves and duties.

Was the shamisen a living art or a dead one?

Without the unfair feudal systems, the music wouldn't be around today to be played the same way it had been four hundred years ago. We could never see into the past without it. Perhaps that was the point. It was a stable system, holding you in place, like stars in a constellation. You alone could connect the dots.

Was the music any less real for its artifice?

I couldn't say.

The stuffed deer head mounted on the wall is no longer alive, but it is preserved, and in its lifelike presence, lasts far longer. But only things that die can go on forever.

≡

Our lessons got lighter, though sometimes, during a pause for corrections, or coming back from a bathroom break, Sensei would take advantage of the *ma* to tell me again how Gautam was a "stinky guy." I cringed and then bit my tongue. To defend would be to deny, and that was the root of my troubles.

I packed my things. Made some decisions. Interviewed one last expert in the lobby of the Imperial Hotel. *Cosmo Japan* appeared on the stands with a feature article on me as one of five foreign women learning traditional arts.

"So bad," Sensei said. "You are leaving and you are going to be famous."

I bought several copies and peered at the pictures of me, arms aloft in a drum strike, at home practicing shamisen, relaxing with the dogs, teaching at school. Sensei appeared smaller, in the corner pictures, off to the right.

What came next was very private and I have, until now, not told anyone about it. I was sitting on the floor of my room in Tokyo during this time, under the skylight, with the sounds of my roommate downstairs feeding the dogs. All of my kimono, scores, tapes, and music were on a ship sailing for America, to be reclaimed there in six weeks.

It was not a glamorous moment, there was no golden halo. The transformation I yearned for did not hit me as the overtaking or ravishing I sought. It was like applying over many years a gentle pressure on a door that was stuck and now finally it gently cracked open. *Would I be shopping until I died? Think of myself my whole life? When would I start thinking of others?*

My fear of making mistakes had kept me in a cycle of selfishness, in endless need for approval. I needed others to tell me who I was and what I wanted. Maybe the part that was missing in me—the howling unfillable hole—was the part of myself that I could only know by tending to others, by thinking about something other than myself.

In my race to become an expert, a transformation had taken place, but not in the way I had imagined. Sensei did not bestow a jeweled pope-like hand and anoint me. It had come from within, at great cost, and it had come out of my own past, even as I tried to escape it. My mistake was not wanting to change, but to *be* changed.

Each mistake was obvious. Each was a teacher. Mastery lay not in mystery, in finding something that was not there, but in learning to use what was.

≡

An achiness haunted me in this new state, a life sheared of veils, and I felt raw, peeled open. Ordering a bowl of noodles, paying my train fare. Everything slowed down and my steps were deliberate again, as if landing anew on the ground. But the ache was also accompanied by a freeing sensation, a lightness that countered its gravity. For the first time in a long time, I was no longer hiding or performing. I had failed, and now when that hot pain shot through me I felt better than I had in a very long time.

I felt like I did in those first days waking in Japan: Where am I? What are those smells? Those sounds? What time is it where I come from? The disorientation tingled, like the prickles in my legs when coming out of numbing *seiza*.

I went to the public bath in Sangenjaya and tried to get clean. While I was soaping outside the tub, feeling sad and sorry for myself, the *obaasan* from the counter walked across the wet tiles and held out a nylon checkered pouch. *"Kare no wasuremono."*

It was Alan's dopp kit, forgotten during our visit to the baths in August. I took the pouch from her and looked inside. There was Alan's slim bar of soap, a yellow disposable razor.

I had never been here before, not even within music as a girl, listening to my Glenn Gould tapes, feeling the *ba-pa-bam* in my legs as I came up the stairs after a piano lesson, alive and in tune.

Not since I was a very young girl, lifting Aunt Sara's seashell by the door, holding its spiky body to my ear and listening to the whoosh of waves, my own heart beating in the primordial swirl. In that swoon and longing, I learned there was something deep inside of me that was not the world but was of it, and that me and that world, we were separate and we were also one.

≡

All that fall, I packed my rooms and shipped boxes to the States. It was nearing the end of 1999 and everybody was worried about the computer systems jamming on the eve of Y2K. I went home for the holidays to see Alan and our families, and returned in January to leave my job and say goodbye.

Throughout all of it, my shamisen lessons continued. Life didn't stop, why should music? Sensei began lessons with me in *hikiutai*, singing to accompany oneself on the shamisen. This was never done in performance, only to teach. She did not sanction me to teach, or tell me I should, she said nothing in fact, only flattened the score of *Suehirogari* with the heel of her palm and waited for me to follow.

It was hard to keep the voice and shamisen strands separate. They kept collapsing into unison, my voice veering toward the shamisen, the shamisen toward the voice.

"Make them chase each other," she said. "You know this music."

On breaks for tea and meals, she called my leaving an "intermission" and said that I could come back any time and she would be waiting.

"You need your own life."

So why was Sensei teaching me *hikiutai* now, on the verge of my going, when it required many more lessons to learn? Was she teaching it because it was so very hard and she wanted me to understand just how accomplished she really was? Or was this another seduction, starting something so difficult that I would have to come back to complete it with her in the future?

I couldn't know. My struggles were just beginning. I would go home first and take care of myself, and then I might be able to return and take care of others.

It meant leaving Sensei and her music room, arriving fresh on a Saturday morning with a bundle of purpose in my backpack for some work to do together, perhaps a drum lesson, a shamisen rehearsal, a concert to steal secrets from the masters. Anywhere, at any time, a bit of wisdom might leak out, something might be learned, and I would not be here to hear it. The desire had pulled me up and forward for years. I had to find out my own desires now.

It meant the end of awaiting her latest plot at the kitchen table while she fed dumplings and fish into the toaster oven with long wooden chopsticks, turning the pieces over as she turned over possibilities for performance in her mind. It meant the end of magic time: the days before performance when she watched over me for paper cuts and train steps, when she dressed me in a new kimono and turned me to the mirror to see.

But it was also the end of a crippling shame, of letting her take care of me, of frustration with her stubborn unwillingness to change, to hear anyone else's ideas, to truly share her world. I didn't want exile or radical solitude. I wanted connection. I wanted to learn how to feel free with my own kind, with a man I loved, with family and friends, unspool the parts of me I'd kept hidden inside.

The end of politely nodding and bowing at her side when I could not understand what was going on, and waiting patiently to be told. I would always need her here. In Japan, I would always be gaijin: distant, excused.

I thought this meant saying goodbye to the odd-shaped shamisen, with its shiny neck, sandalwood pegs, and silk strings. But really, it meant saying goodbye to an illusion that it was conquerable. There was much more to it than I'd realized. Timing. Confidence. Discipline. Years I didn't have.

And so on and on, Sensei and I went, untwisting the braid of shamisen and voice. Off and asymmetric, they fit by not fitting. By sliding loosely and slyly, waving, but never landing. The interplay was everything. Do not seek unison. Do not fall into line. Do not attempt to fit in.

"Don't belong to me," she seemed to be saying. "Belong to yourself."

=

And then it was time.

On my last night I stood in Sensei's *genkan*. She was sitting on the threshold between rooms and I was lacing my shoes. We'd performed this ritual hundreds of times after lessons and concerts, before returning to the much harder work of the living in between music.

"Your return is like *Canton* story," she said, recalling Alan's story of the foreigner waking up and finding out he has dreamed Japan.

"It's not a dream, Sensei. It's real."

"A dream needs at least two people." She smiled.

"You and me. That's two."

"But we are human, Janet. Experience is not so strong after long time."

She began ruminating about a new student and I stopped listening for a moment. I was nervous, wondering how we would say goodbye, if she would cry, or I would, if I would slip out with a joke as I had so many times to assuage the fear that when I returned she would be gone.

And then she was shaking her head. "Doesn't make sense, human beings."

I looked up from her sink full of teacups, the dust-tufted spices, the lacquered bowl of snacks on her kitchen table. And through the doorway, the shamisen hanging on the wall in colorful silk covers.

"If you think about it, nothing makes sense," she said, looking at me.

"What are you talking about?"

"You and me, why should we meet?"

"Kismet. Fate," I said.

"Really no sense, nothing."

The dusky kitchen, the ugly brown linoleum, the flaking concrete.

Almost four years earlier, I was just as scared and unsure where I was headed. She'd put a shamisen on my lap, some strings that I could strum, and that had started it all. I learned this: all you had to do was get moving and then something would happen, anything, and that was all right.

She rose and leaned her tiny frame into me and I felt the bones of her arms and lots of space all around. "Go so you can come back. As long as we are healthy, we can play music."

Outside the sun was sinking low as I turned onto Lucky Seven

Boulevard, the strip I'd walked hundreds of times to play music. This time my hands were empty: no music, no bags of eggs, no *nashi* pears, no *mikan*, no *sakura mochi*, no piece of her to consume and nourish me. *Tebura*: "empty hands," a phrase she taught me for when you returned from a trip without souvenirs for people. The ritual gift meant "we are connected," "you are in my thoughts." It was stronger than saying, "I like you." Or "I love you." It was real and in the world.

Three golden strings, the impossibly long neck hiding its secrets, the cat skin, and the sad sound, all mine and always beyond. There was nothing to hold onto.

I was no master. I knew nothing.

It was a relief.

Afterword

Certain names and circumstances have been changed to disguise the identities of those involved. My story is mine alone, as well as its errors, mistakes, and flaws. I am not an expert on Japan or the shamisen or anyone else in my story. The work is interpretive, sometimes to the extreme, which to me, was very much a part of my experience in Japan.

To protect my teacher, I have called her Sensei, which is a name she did not want to be called. She is aware of this, and approves, knowing its irony. I last saw her in the winter of 2018 in Tokyo. I performed with her group at an international festival in Meguro. We performed in chairs, thank goodness, and were joined by an impressive group of Japanese professionals. Time has brought compromise.

She was living in a studio condo she had bought recently. The one room looked out on Tokyo Tower, and on a good day, a view of Mount Fuji. It was like living on a postage stamp on one of the world's most beautiful postcards. Since 3/11, the day in 2011 when the earthquake and tsunami hit Fukushima and northern Japan, her teaching has dwindled.

One day, as we were crossing a street near her place, I told her of the moniker I wanted to use for her in the book. We had been spending afternoons at family restaurants over my manuscript binder, checking dates and facts. I read aloud portions so she would understand. I chose the word Sensei because I still didn't know what else to call her.

"Teacher!" she said. "Really ... that is our relationship?"

"Of course it is," I said, exasperated. And then, "No, of course not."

She tilted her head. "Teacher ..."

Later in the trip, during one of our manuscript sessions, she told me, "I thought back then, you, Alan, Kenneth, very talented students. I thought it was normal."

Students came less often now. Few bought shamisen. Who knew how many concerts she had left in her?

"Back then, I had no idea what I was doing," she said. She shook her head. "Not at all."

Acknowledgments

A work such as this, about an art such as this, contains the help and guidance of more people than I will ever be able to formally recognize, but I want to thank here the many who have supported this work and helped bring it into the world: Peter Goodman at Stone Bridge Press, for his patience and generous feedback, the third time's a charm; Michael Palmer, the coolest publicist ever; Linda Ronan for her graceful cover design; Mary Bisbee-Beek, for recommending my work to Peter; Charles Everitt, an early reader and supporter; Rachel Manley, mentor and Sensei's greatest fan; other writing mentors, Wayne Brown, Alexandra Johnson, Kathleen Spivack, Rachel Simon, and Vivian Gornick, each of whose deft edits contributed to this story; Gish Jen, who said, *Of course, it's about both of you*; Charlotte Silver for her superb editing, shirtwaists, and the coffees at Café Algiers; Steven Cramer and Jana Van der Veer, my longstanding colleagues at Lesley; Pamela Petro, kindred spirit since that first coffee in Northampton; Meenakshi Chhabra, for her clarifying conversations about non-Western learning; Donald Richie, friend and constant supporter; Curtis Patterson, dear friend and musical mate; Denise Henry, loyal *senpai* and friend; Chie-sensei, Kikuyu-sensei, Wakatsuki-sensei, who taught me how to respect art, and myself; Yamagishi-sensei, for giving me the words; my cousin Suzi, who listened as I read pages aloud to her in her kitchen one cold December eve; my Aunt Sara, who believed in the arts, and in me; Naomi, Jon, Kinoa, and Denali, for hospitality and friendship; Tamami, for the fortunes; Tayloe Denton, who always told me to write; Jenn O'Neil, whose Sunday night calls started it all; Erin

Leiman, for her laughter and blue pencil over a decade of friendship; Sarah Kilgallon, for supporting the "little bits" and reminding me that ambivalence is deadly; Wesley Savick, for his belief in me, and for telling me that a writer needs a cardigan; Jay and Mami Keister and William Malm, who helped me learn; Howard Norman and Jane Shore, for renting me their Vermont farmhouse in the winter of 2014 and telling me that a writer needs an address; the writers' group at the cottage, Molly Power, Liz Knapp, and Karen Vatz; Barbara Baig, for the conversations about writing; Colin, Matt, Chris, Nancy, Carlos and Ryan, my best and only group; the women at Miracles on Monday, and most of all Renee, who stayed; friends at the Adamant Co-op; the Vermont Studio Center for an Artist's Residency in May 2017; Turkey Land Cove Foundation for an Artist's Residency in September 2017; the brothers of the Society of Saint John the Evangelist, for their faith and their hermitage; Dr. Lowe, without whom I never would have finished; the Boston Graduate School of Psychoanalysis, for helping me stay; The Writers' Room of Boston, for welcoming me to their tribe; the Japan Society of Boston, the JET New England Teachers Alumni Association, the Hanami Club of UMass-Boston, Showa Boston, the Peabody-Essex Museum, Mariko Itoh, Roger Keyes, and anyone else who invited me to me play shamisen, in Japan or America, and especially the group under the hemlocks and over the falls; for all students and fellow players I have met over the years and gave me joy in sharing this music; Cici and Miss Mollie, who kept me company; my parents, Sam and Millie, who were always there for me; my brother John, for his humor and constant respite; and for Sensei, thank you, always, for taking a chance on me and for the golden time.

JP